# Visual Art
## for the secondary grades

Kerrian Neu

The materials in this book may be reproduced for personal or classroom use only. The reproduction of any part of this publication for an entire school or school system is strictly prohibited. No part of this publication may be transmitted, stored, or recorded in any form without written permission from the author. For more information regarding permissions and other books by this author, visit www.sVisualArt.com.

© 2011 Kerrian Neu. All rights reserved.

Writing, design and illustration by Kerrian Neu.

ISBN        1-46355-881-3
ISBN-13   978-1-463-55881-9

kerrian neu design
print/web design & illustration

www.tahoekerri.com
www.svisualart.com
www.benthebee.com
www.evisualart.com

## INTRODUCTION.

This book contains over 60 visual art lessons and most integrate art history with art creation, covering art movements, artists and their work, and the numerous techniques used. Students learn about color theory, the elements and principles of art and drawing techniques before creating works of art using various art techniques and styles. Students learn to analyze art and develop their own portfolios. The California visual art standards are addressed and those used in each area are listed by area or movement in the appendix. National visual art standards are also all covered, but not listed.

## AREAS OF STUDY.

This book is divided into ten areas, covering art basics and techniques, art movements and their artists, two and three dimensional art creation and analysis.

Lessons should begin with the color theory area. A basic understanding of mixing colors is a must to become a better artist. Students mix complements and tints, tones and shades, in addition to the color wheel. The elements and principles area follows the color theory area and it discusses both. Students need this knowledge to critique and compose art.

The drawing area introduces students to various drawing techniques. These techniques will be used in all other areas, as students sketch and draw their ideas before painting or sculpting.

There are four two-dimensional art areas. These should be taught in the order presented in this book. The first three areas cover several art movements and their artists. Movements start with Realism and continue through Impressionism, Post Impressionism, Fauvism, Cubism, Surrealism, Contemporary Art and finish with Pop Art. Students create their own art based on techniques and characteristics of those movements. The last two-dimensional area covers printmaking and basic black and white photography techniques. Artists Edvard Munch, William Henry Fox Talbot and Ansel Adams are also introduced.

There are two three-dimensional art areas. The first covers pottery and woodcarving techniques while introducing Minoan pottery and Oceania wood art. The second covers mosaics and the Earth Art movement. The beginnings of mosaics and artists of the Earth Art movement are also discussed.

The final area covers the creation of student portfolios and the critical analysis of the works of well-known artists and the students. Students discuss what should be art, learn how to analyze their art and reflect on the creation of art.

# Visual Art for the secondary grades — page 3

## Contents

- Additional Information .................................................... page 4
- Color Theory .............................................................. page 5
- Elements and Principles .................................................. page 17
- Drawing .................................................................. page 27
- Two Dimensional Art 1 .................................................... page 37
  - Realism ............................................................... page 38
  - Impressionism ......................................................... page 42
  - Post Impressionism .................................................... page 48
- Two Dimensional Art 2 .................................................... page 55
  - Fauvism ............................................................... page 56
  - Cubism ................................................................ page 60
  - Surrealism ............................................................ page 64
- Two Dimensional Art 3 .................................................... page 71
  - Contemporary Art ...................................................... page 72
  - Pop Art ............................................................... page 75
- Two Dimensional Art 4 .................................................... page 81
  - Printmaking ........................................................... page 82
  - Photography ........................................................... page 85
- Three Dimensional Art 1 .................................................. page 91
  - Pottery ............................................................... page 92
  - Wood Carving .......................................................... page 95
- Three Dimensional Art 2 .................................................. page 99
  - Mosaics ............................................................... page 100
  - Earth Art ............................................................. page 103
- Analysis and Portfolio ................................................... page 109
- Appendix ................................................................. page 117
  - Timeline of Artists ................................................... page 118
  - Index of Artists ...................................................... page 119
  - Movement/Art Worksheet ................................................ page 120
  - References ............................................................ page 121
  - State Standards ....................................................... page 122

# Additional Information

page 4 — VISUAL ART for the secondary grades

## MEDIA.
The art creation lessons offer opportunities to learn and experiment with various techniques. Although oil painting is not included, it can be substituted for acrylic painting. Oils take a long time to dry, require various additives as well as turpentine. Acrylics create similar effects as oils, but dry quickly and are easy to work with and clean up.

MEDIA USED:
Acrylic paints, black and white photography, charcoal, clay, collage, colored pencils, earthworks, encaustic paints, hand coloring, india inks, linocuts, markers, mosaics, pen and ink, pencils, scratchboard, screenprinting, soft pastels, sunprinting, tempera, watercolors and wood.

## THE INSIDE ART BINDER.
Each student needs to have a binder to keep all worksheets. Beginning with the color theory worksheets, they are for students to reference the different movements and the artists, techniques, color behaviors and principles and elements of art. Binders should be kept in the classroom.

## SKETCHBOOKS AND COMPLETION OF WORK.
If possible, students should have a sketchbook to draw their ideas and to practice their own techniques. After completing their assignments, they can draw in their sketchbooks or be allowed to create their own art. Completed art should be put into student portfolios.

## GRADING RUBRICS.
Each area includes a grading rubric for each student. Not all lessons are included on the rubric, just the art creation and analysis lessons. In addition to the lessons, student attendance is included. Students are deducted points for absences, tardies and for leaving a dirty work area. Quizzes are included in the color theory area and the elements and principles area rubrics. Also included are areas for comments and a grading scale.

## SUPPLEMENTAL MATERIALS.
Lessons that present artists require viewing of their work. These supplemental (full color) materials are available at www.sVisualArt.com for online viewing or free download for classroom use.

# COLOR THEORY

Color Terms . . . . . . . . . . . . . . . . . . . . . . . . . . . . . . . . . . . . . . . . . . . . . . . . . . . . . page 6

Area Guide . . . . . . . . . . . . . . . . . . . . . . . . . . . . . . . . . . . . . . . . . . . . . . . . . . . . page 7

Area Worksheets

    Defining Color Terms . . . . . . . . . . . . . . . . . . . . . . . . . . . . . . . . . . . . . . . page 9

    Mixing the Color Wheel . . . . . . . . . . . . . . . . . . . . . . . . . . . . . . . . . . . . page 10

    Mixing Tints, Shades and Tones . . . . . . . . . . . . . . . . . . . . . . . . . . . . . page 11

    Mixing of the Color Complements . . . . . . . . . . . . . . . . . . . . . . . . . . . page 12

    Color Harmonies . . . . . . . . . . . . . . . . . . . . . . . . . . . . . . . . . . . . . . . . . page 13

Color Terms Quiz . . . . . . . . . . . . . . . . . . . . . . . . . . . . . . . . . . . . . . . . . . . . page 14

Grading Rubric . . . . . . . . . . . . . . . . . . . . . . . . . . . . . . . . . . . . . . . . . . . . . . page 16

# Color Terms

### Primary Colors
Colors that can not be made by mixing other colors; red, yellow and blue.

### Secondary Colors
Colors made by mixing two primary colors; orange, green and purple.

### Tertiary Colors
Colors made by mixing a primary color with a secondary color; red-orange, yellow-orange, yellow-green, blue-green, blue-purple, red-purple.

### Complementary Colors
Colors that are opposites on the color wheel and create neutral colors when mixed together.

### Tint
Color mixed with white.

### Shade
Color mixed with black.

### Tone
Color mixed with gray.

### Analogous Color Harmony
Any three colors next to each other on the color wheel.

### Split Complement Color Harmony
A color and the two analogous colors to its complement.

### Triad Color Harmony
Three evenly spaced colors on the color wheel which form an equilateral triangle.

### Tetradic - Square Color Harmony
Four evenly spaced colors on the color wheel which form a square.

### Tetradic - Rectangle Color Harmony
Two pairs of complementary colors which form a rectangle.

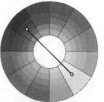
COMPLEMENT

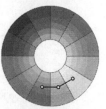
ANALOGOUS

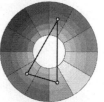
SPLIT COMPLEMENT

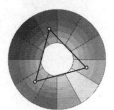
TRIAD

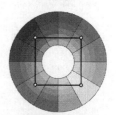
TETRADIC - SQUARE

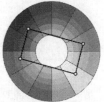
TETRADIC - RECTANGLE

## INTRODUCTION.
Learning about color, its harmonies and how color mixes are important to the visual arts. Color defines what we see and understanding color produces better quality and better representation of color in works of art.

## AREA OBJECTIVES.
To experiment with color. Students will discover how color behaves when mixed with white, black and gray. They will create new colors by mixing complementary colors. Students will learn about color harmonies and organize the color section of their Inside Art Binder.

## SUPPLIES NEEDED.
Tempera in red, yellow, blue, black and white, brushes, water, palettes, pencils, color theory area worksheets, Inside Art Binder, color quiz.

## MEDIA USED.
Tempera

## AREA LESSONS.

### Defining the Color Terms
1. Pass out the "Defining the Color Terms" worksheet, and discuss the color terms.
2. Students list the terms and write the definitions of each term.
3. Save worksheet for the Inside Art Binder.

### Mixing the Color Wheel
1. Review the color wheel, primary colors, and how to mix the secondary and tertiary colors.
2. Pass out the "Mixing the Color Wheel" worksheet, paints, brushes, palettes and water. Students use only red, yellow and blue to mix the rest of the colors.
3. Students should paint the primary colors first, the secondary colors next, and then finally the tertiary colors.
4. Save worksheet for the Inside Art Binder.

### Mixing Tints, Shades and Tones
1. Pass out one "Mixing Tints, Shades and Tones" worksheet and supplies needed to each student.
2. Students use one worksheet for one color, which they mix with white, black and gray. They will need six worksheets to paint all the primary and secondary colors.
3. Save worksheets for the Inside Art Binder.

# Area Guide - Color Theory

## Mixing the Color Complements

When you mix complementary colors, they produce neutral colors. Ultimately, equal parts of each complementary color cancel each other, producing gray. Since we rarely use pure pigments, gray is not produced, but many variations of neutral colors are.

1. Pass out the "Mixing the Color Complements" worksheet and supplies needed.
2. Do not demonstrate how to complete the worksheet, only instruct the students to mix the complementary colors in the order the worksheet shows.
3. Save worksheet for the Inside Art Binder.
4. Take the complements a step farther. Students choose one neutral from each complement pair and complete a tint, shade and tone worksheet for each, creating six more worksheets.

## Color Harmonies

Color harmonies are used to create unique effects to viewers eye. Harmonies work together to communicate moods and ideas.

1. Using a color wheel, discuss the definitions of the color harmonies. Students can refer to their definition page as well as their color wheel.
2. Pass out the "Color Harmonies" worksheet and supplies needed, telling students to produce the harmonies with the colors of their choosing.
3. Save worksheet for the Inside Art Binder.

## Color Quiz

1. Allow students time to review the color terms and definitions.
2. Pass out the "Color Quiz" to each student.
3. Collect and score quizzes.
4. Students review their scores.

Answers to quiz: **1.** Green, orange and purple. **2.** A tint is a color mixed with white. **3.** Tertiary colors are made by mixing a primary color with a secondary color. **4.** Three colors that are next to each other on the color wheel - example: red, red-orange, red-purple. **5.** Primary colors are colors that can not be made by mixing other colors. **6.** A shade is a color mixed with black. **7.** Any two of the six complement pairs. Red and green, yellow and purple, blue and orange, red-orange and blue-green, yellow-orange and blue-purple, yellow-green and red-purple. **8.** A triad color harmony is three colors evenly spaced on the color wheel which form a equilateral triangle. **9.** A split complement harmony is a color and the two analogous colors to it's complement - example: yellow, blue-purple and red-purple. **10.** A tone is a color mixed with gray.

# Define the Color Terms

Name _____

Write and define each of the color terms below.

| TERM | DEFINITION |
|------|------------|
|      |            |
|      |            |
|      |            |
|      |            |
|      |            |
|      |            |
|      |            |
|      |            |
|      |            |
|      |            |
|      |            |

# COLOR WHEEL

Name _____

- RED
- RED-ORANGE
- ORANGE
- ORANGE-YELLOW
- YELLOW
- YELLOW-GREEN
- GREEN
- GREEN-BLUE
- BLUE
- BLUE-VIOLET
- VIOLET
- VIOLET-RED

Color Theory — Mixing the Color Wheel — page 10

VISUAL ART
for the secondary grades

# Tints, Shades and Tones

Name _____

| 100% HUE | 90/10 | 80/20 | 70/30 | 60/40 | 50/50 | 40/60 | 30/70 | 20/80 | 10/90 | 100% WHITE |
|---|---|---|---|---|---|---|---|---|---|---|
|  |  |  |  |  |  |  |  |  |  |  |

| 100% HUE | 90/10 | 80/20 | 70/30 | 60/40 | 50/50 | 40/60 | 30/70 | 20/80 | 10/90 | 100% GRAY |
|---|---|---|---|---|---|---|---|---|---|---|
|  |  |  |  |  |  |  |  |  |  |  |

| 100% HUE | 90/10 | 80/20 | 70/30 | 60/40 | 50/50 | 40/60 | 30/70 | 20/80 | 10/90 | 100% BLACK |
|---|---|---|---|---|---|---|---|---|---|---|
|  |  |  |  |  |  |  |  |  |  |  |

VISUAL ART for the secondary grades — Color Theory — Mixing Tints, Shades and Tones

# COLOR COMPLEMENTS

Name _____

| 100% RED | 75% RED  25% GREEN | 50% RED  50% GREEN | 25% RED  75% GREEN | 100% GREEN |

| 100% RED-ORANGE | 75% RED-ORANGE  25% GREEN-BLUE | 50% RED-ORANGE  50% GREEN-BLUE | 25% RED-ORANGE  75% GREEN-BLUE | 100% GREEN-BLUE |

| 100% ORANGE | 75% ORANGE  25% BLUE | 50% ORANGE  50% BLUE | 25% ORANGE  75% BLUE | 100% BLUE |

| 100% ORANGE-YELLOW | 75% ORANGE-YELLOW  25% BLUE-PURPLE | 50% ORANGE-YELLOW  50% BLUE-PURPLE | 25% ORANGE-YELLOW  75% BLUE-PURPLE | 100% BLUE-PURPLE |

| 100% YELLOW | 75% YELLOW  25% PURPLE | 50% YELLOW  50% PURPLE | 25% YELLOW  75% PURPLE | 100% PURPLE |

| 100% YELLOW-GREEN | 75% YELLOW-GREEN  25% PURPLE-RED | 50% YELLOW-GREEN  50% PURPLE-RED | 25% YELLOW-GREEN  75% PURPLE-RED | 100% PURPLE-RED |

Color Theory — Mixing of the Color Complements

VISUAL ART
for the secondary grades

# COLOR HARMONIES

Name _____

Complementary

Complementary

Complementary

Complementary

Complementary

Complementary

Analogous

Analogous

Split Complement

Split Complement

Triad

Triad

Tetradic - Square

Tetradic - Square

Tetradic - Rectangle

Tetradic - Rectangle

**visual art** for the secondary grades | page 13 | Color Theory | Color Harmonies

# COLOR QUIZ

Name _____

Answer the questions below. 2 points per question, 20 possible points.

1. List the secondary colors.
   _____

2. What is a tint?
   _____

3. How are tertiary colors made?
   _____
   _____

4. List three colors that make an analogous harmony.
   _____

5. What is the definition of primary colors?
   _____
   _____

6. What is a shade?
   _____

7. List two complementary pairs.
   _____
   _____

8. What is the definition of the triad color harmony?
   _____
   _____

9. List three colors that make a split complement harmony.
   _____

10. What is a tone?
    _____

# COLOR QUIZ

Name _____

Answer in complete sentences. 10 possible points.

Recalling your mixing of color complements, describe what happened when you mixed one pair of colors. Be sure to include: what did you expect would happen? what was actually produced? how can you use the results in future works of art?

_____
_____
_____
_____
_____
_____
_____
_____
_____
_____
_____
_____
_____
_____
_____
_____
_____
_____
_____
_____
_____
_____
_____

| PERIOD | STUDENT NAME | TOTAL POINTS | GRADE |

| LESSON POINTS | QUIZ POINTS | ATTENDANCE POINTS |
|---|---|---|
| _____ [90] | _____ [30] | 30 - _____ = _____<br>TOTAL MINUS DEDUCTIONS |

| LESSON | PARTICIPATION | COMPLETION | QUALITY | TOTAL POINTS |
|---|---|---|---|---|
| Defining Color Terms | 1 2 3 4 5 | 1 2 3 4 5 | 1 2 3 4 5 | _____ |
| Mixing the Color Wheel | 1 2 3 4 5 | 1 2 3 4 5 | 1 2 3 4 5 | _____ |
| Mixing Tints, Shades and Tones | 2 4 6 8 10 | 2 4 6 8 10 | 2 4 6 8 10 | _____ |
| Mixing of the Color Complements | 1 2 3 4 5 | 1 2 3 4 5 | 1 2 3 4 5 | _____ |
| Color Harmonies | 1 2 3 4 5 | 1 2 3 4 5 | 1 2 3 4 5 | _____ |

Participation: was the student a part of discussions, worked throughout class.
Completion: student's work - did they follow directions, finish assignments.
Quality: is the work carefully created, well thought-out, show self-expression.

## Attendance
Daily recording, marking late or absent and workspace/materials cleaned and stored. L=late. A=absent. ✓=clean workspace.

8/21
A
✓

**ATTENDANCE DEDUCTIONS**
#of Late =____ x ____ = ____   #of Absent =____   #of Dirty space =____   Total =____

**150 TOTAL POINTS**
- A  = 150-140
- A- = 139-135
- B+ = 134-131
- B  = 130-125
- B- = 124-120
- C+ = 119-116
- C  = 115-110
- C- = 109-105
- D+ = 104-101
- D  = 100-95
- D- = 94-90

Color Theory — Grading Rubric — page 16

VISUAL ART
for the secondary grades

# ELEMENTS and PRINCIPLES

Elements of Art . . . . . . . . . . . . . . . . . . . . . . . . . . . . . . . . . . . . . . . . . . . . page 18

Principles of Art . . . . . . . . . . . . . . . . . . . . . . . . . . . . . . . . . . . . . . . . . . . page 19

Area Guide . . . . . . . . . . . . . . . . . . . . . . . . . . . . . . . . . . . . . . . . . . . . . . page 20

Area Worksheets

    Defining Elements of Art Terms . . . . . . . . . . . . . . . . . . . . . . . . . . page 22

    Defining Principles of Art Terms . . . . . . . . . . . . . . . . . . . . . . . . . . page 23

Elements and Principles of Art Quiz . . . . . . . . . . . . . . . . . . . . . . . . . . . page 24

Grading Rubric . . . . . . . . . . . . . . . . . . . . . . . . . . . . . . . . . . . . . . . . . . page 26

# Elements of Art

### Color.
Color is the visual perception of the spectrum of light. Three properties of color are: hue, intensity and value. Hue is pure color [except for white and black], and creates moods like warm and cool. Intensity ranges from dull to vivid. Value ranges from light to dark.

### Form.
A three-dimensional figure that has mass and a height, width and depth.

### Line.
A continuous mark that defines space, outlines, or creates movement or texture.

### Shape.
Geometric or organic enclosed flat [two-dimensional] spaces with a length and width and are bounded by other elements of art.

### Space.
The creation of a feeling of depth or three-dimensions sometimes through the use of positives and negatives, color or size of objects.

### Texture.
The surface quality of an object. They can be optical or tactile and are rough, soft, hard, smooth, bumpy, coarse, etc.

### Value.
Value refers to lightness or darkness of a color with high value colors being close to white and low value colors being close to black. Tints are created by adding white to a color. Shades are created by adding black to a color.

## Principles of Art

### Balance.
Balance makes a work of art comfortable, with a sense of unity and calmness. Lack of balance can be upsetting to the viewer. There are three types of balance: symmetrical [bilateral] - both sides appear the same; asymmetrical - balance is not equal or even; and radial - equal length from a central axis.

### Emphasis.
The creation of a focal point [or points] that attract the viewer's eye.

### Movement.
The path of the viewer's eye through a work of art. It is created through the use of rhythm of elements, contrast, and emphasis.

### Proportion.
The perception of size and the relationships of size within a work of art. The golden mean/ratio and the Fibonacci series are ways to create pleasing proportion.

### Rhythm.
The movement throughout a work of art. Created by the use of repetition of patterns, color, size, shapes, lines and forms. Rhythm can make a work seem alive.

### Unity.
The controlling of variety. Unity gives the feeling of completeness to a work of art. It can be achieved through the harmony of color, texture or material and the repetition of like objects, shapes or forms.

### Variety.
The difference between elements in a work of art, which shows contrast. The contrast of the elements can be created by using light against dark, rough against smooth, small against large, and complementary colors.

# Area Guide - Elements & Principles

*page 20 — Visual Art for the secondary grades*

## INTRODUCTION.
To be able to discuss, critique and compose visual art, one needs an understanding of the elements and principles of art. This area defines the elements as: color, form, line, shape, space, texture and value; and the principles as: balance, emphasis, movement, proportion, rhythm, unity and variety. Elements of art are used to create art and help make the principles of art, which in turn, are used to create visual pleasing, unique and beautiful art. All artists use the elements and principles of art in their work.

## AREA OBJECTIVES.
To understand, use and discuss the elements and principles of art. Students will define and draw the seven elements of art, and use them to create a work of art. Students will define and draw the seven principles of art, and use them to create a work of art. Students will discuss the elements and principles of art, reviewing their own and their classmates' work.

## SUPPLIES NEEDED.
Markers, tempera, or colored pencils, drawing pencils, strips of paper at least 14 inches long, 12x18 inch sheets of blank paper, elements and principles worksheets, Inside Art Binder, elements and principles quiz.

## MEDIA USED.
Markers, tempera or colored pencils

## AREA LESSONS.

### The Elements of Art
1. Pass out "The Elements Defined" worksheet, explaining the importance of the elements [i.e. they make up all art and the principles of art, they are needed to produce art].
2. List, define, discuss and draw the elements of art. Students fill-in the worksheet while discussing and can also draw examples as a part of their definitions.
3. Pass out blank white strips of paper, and have students divide it into seven spaces.
4. Instruct students to draw and color representations of the seven elements.
5. Display elements and insert "The Elements Defined" worksheet in the students' Inside Art Binder.

### Using the Elements
1. Students retrieve their element definition worksheet to use as a reference to create their piece.
2. Explain and display what the students need to do for their art. They need to choose at least four elements to create an abstract work of art. It can be based on a landscape scene or objects, but it doesn't have to be. The main goal is to use the elements.

3. Students sketch their ideas before creating their final work.
4. Pass out 12x18 sheets of blank paper and allow students to use markers, tempera or colored pencils to create their work.
5. Display and discuss student works. Be sure to find the elements in each work.

## The Principles of Art

1. Pass out "The Principles Defined" worksheet, explaining the importance of the principles [i.e. they are used to create visually pleasing art].
2. List, define, discuss and draw the principles of art. Students fill-in the worksheet while discussing and can also draw examples as a part of their definitions.
3. Pass out blank white strips of paper, and have students divide it into seven spaces.
4. Instruct students to draw and color representations of the seven principles.
5. Display principles and insert "The Principles Defined" worksheet in the students' Inside Art Binder.

## Using the Principles

1. Students retrieve their principle definition worksheet to use as a reference to create their piece.
2. Explain and display what the students need to do for their art. They need to choose at least four principles to create an abstract work of art. It can be based on a landscape scene or objects, [but it doesn't have to be.] The main goal is to use the principles.
3. Students sketch their ideas before creating their final work.
4. Pass out 12x18 sheets of blank paper and allow students to use markers, tempera or colored pencils to create their work.
5. Display and discuss student works. Be sure to find the principles and even the elements in each work.

## Elements and Principles Quiz

1. Allow students time to review the elements and principles of art.
2. Pass out the "Elements and Principles Quiz" to each student.
3. Collect and score quizzes.
4. Students review their scores.

Answers to quiz: 1. Color, form, line, shape, space, texture and value.  2. Balance, emphasis, movement, proportion, rhythm, unity and value.  3. Value refers to lightness or darkness of a color with high value colors being close to white and low value colors being close to black.  4. A shape is a two-dimensional or flat enclosed space. A form is a three-dimensional figure that has mass.  5. Proportion is the perception of size and the relationships of size within a work of art.  6. Unity gives the feeling of completeness to a work of art.  7. Three properties of color are: hue, intensity and value.
8. Elements that can be used to create rhythm are: patterns, color, size, shapes, lines and forms.
9. Three types of balance are: symmetrical [bilateral], asymmetrical and radial.

# ELEMENTS OF ART

Name _____

Write and define each of the elements of art below.

| ELEMENT | DEFINITION |
|---|---|
|  |  |
|  |  |
|  |  |
|  |  |
|  |  |
|  |  |
|  |  |

Elements & Principles — The Elements Defined

# PRINCIPLES OF ART

Name _____

Write and define each of the principles of art below.

| PRINCIPLE | DEFINITION |
|---|---|
|  |  |
|  |  |
|  |  |
|  |  |
|  |  |
|  |  |
|  |  |

# ELEMENTS & PRINCIPLES QUIZ

Name _____

Answer the questions below. 2 points per question, except where noted, 21 possible points.

1. List all seven elements of art. [3.5 points]
   _____
   _____

2. List all seven principles of art. [3.5 points]
   _____
   _____

3. Define value.
   _____
   _____

4. What is the difference between a shape and a form?
   _____
   _____

5. Define proportion.
   _____
   _____

6. Why is unity important in art?
   _____
   _____

7. What are the three properties of color?
   _____

8. List two elements of art that can be used to create rhythm.
   _____

9. What are the three types of balance?
   _____
   _____

Elements & Principles    Quiz

# Elements & Principles Quiz

Name: _____

Answer in complete sentences. 9 possible points.

Why is it important to know and understand the elements and principles of art? How can you use the elements and principles of art to improve your art creations?

_____
_____
_____
_____
_____
_____
_____
_____
_____
_____
_____
_____
_____
_____
_____
_____
_____
_____
_____
_____

| PERIOD | STUDENT NAME | TOTAL POINTS | GRADE |
|---|---|---|---|

| LESSON POINTS | QUIZ POINTS | ATTENDANCE POINTS |
|---|---|---|
| _____ [90] | _____ [30] | 30 - ____ = _____ <br> TOTAL MINUS DEDUCTIONS |

| LESSON | PARTICIPATION | COMPLETION | QUALITY | TOTAL POINTS |
|---|---|---|---|---|
| Elements of Art - Defining | 1 2 3 4 5 | 1 2 3 4 5 | 1 2 3 4 5 | _____ |
| Drawing | 1 2 3 4 5 | 1 2 3 4 5 | 1 2 3 4 5 | _____ |
| Using the Elements | 1 2 3 4 5 | 1 2 3 4 5 | 1 2 3 4 5 | _____ |
| Principles of Art - Defining | 1 2 3 4 5 | 1 2 3 4 5 | 1 2 3 4 5 | _____ |
| Drawing | 1 2 3 4 5 | 1 2 3 4 5 | 1 2 3 4 5 | _____ |
| Using the Principles | 1 2 3 4 5 | 1 2 3 4 5 | 1 2 3 4 5 | _____ |

Participation: was the student a part of discussions, worked throughout class. Completion: student's work - did they follow directions, finish assignments. Quality: is the work carefully created, well thought-out, show self-expression.

## Attendance

Daily recording, marking late or absent and workspace/materials cleaned and stored. L=late. A=absent. ✓=clean workspace.

8/21
A
✓

| ATTENDANCE DEDUCTIONS |
|---|
| #of Late = ____ x ____ = ____ | #of Absent = ____ | #of Dirty space = ____ | Total = ____ |

**150 TOTAL POINTS**

A  = 150-140
A- = 139-135

B+ = 134-131
B  = 130-125
B- = 124-120

C+ = 119-116
C  = 115-110
C- = 109-105

D+ = 104-101
D  = 100-95
D- = 94-90

Elements & Principles   Grading Rubric

VISUAL ART
for the secondary grades

# DRAWING

| | |
|---|---|
| Drawing Terms | page 28 |
| Area Guide | page 29 |
| Area Worksheets | |
|     Drawing Techniques | page 33 |
| Area Artists | |
|     Leonardo da Vinci | page 34 |
|     Albrecht Dürer | page 35 |
| Grading Rubric | page 36 |

# Drawing Terms

### Drawing.
The depiction of shapes and forms by the use of lines or dots.

### Contour.
Outline drawings, focusing only on the line created by the object viewed. These drawings try to duplicate the line of the object viewed, and generally use one continuous line.

### Blind-Contour.
Outline drawings, done without looking at the paper and use one continuous line.

### Gesture.
A quick sketch typically of the human figure, showing movement and action poses. Sometimes used as a warm-up to exercise observational skills. Usually done in 30 seconds or up to two minutes.

### Hatch.
Creating a series of closely spaced parallel lines used to depict shading and volume.

### Cross-Hatch.
Creating a series of closely spaced parallel lines that intersect each other at a different angle and are used to depict shading and volume.

### Stipple.
Creating a pattern of small dots of one color that depict shape, shading and volume.

### One-Point Perspective.
A drawing with a single vanishing point. Usual depictions are of a road or railroad track.

### Two-Point Perspective.
A drawing with two vanishing points. Usual depictions are of corners of an object or building.

# Area Guide - Drawing

## INTRODUCTION.
Drawing is the first step in creating art, and understanding the various techniques of drawing are important to learn. This area covers basic and more advanced drawing techniques. Leonardo da Vinci and Albrecht Dürer are introduced and discussed.

## AREA OBJECTIVES.
Students will learn about Leonardo da Vinci and Albrecht Dürer, including their lives and their art. Students will experiment with basic drawing techniques - gesture, contour and blind-contour. Students will work to understand the effects of light and represent light by shading objects. Students will create works using one- and two-point perspective. Students will learn and use more advanced techniques of hatching and stippling before creating a final drawing composition using the techniques they have learned.

## SUPPLIES NEEDED.
Newsprint, pencils, charcoal, rulers, objects to view, a spotlight or desk light, fabric to drape, black and white images of animals (available at www.svisualart.com), 6x9, 9x12, 12x15 inch white paper, black ink pens, examples of stippling, Leonardo da Vinci and Albrecht Dürer handouts, examples of their work (available at www.svisualart.com), drawing techniques worksheet, Inside Art Binder.

## MEDIA USED.
Pencil
Charcoal
Pen and Ink

## AREA LESSONS.

### Introduction to Drawing - Leonardo da Vinci

This brief lesson introduces the drawing area. Leonardo da Vinci drew almost 2,500 sketches, some to do studies for his paintings, and others to illustrate inventions or scientific views. Proceed directly to the next lesson after reviewing Leonardo da Vinci.

1. Pass out Leonardo da Vinci handout, read and discuss.
2. View and discuss Leonardo's sketches.

Area Guide - Drawing

## Gesture Drawing

This drawing technique is used by artists to do quick studies of movement and action before creating and composing a work of art.

1. Pass out drawing techniques worksheet and pencils.
   [Once the term is drawn and defined, add worksheet to the Inside Art Binder.]
2. Define gesture drawing.
3. Ask a student to pose, showing action, and demonstrate a gesture drawing. Be sure to be quick, and not include details.
4. Pass out newsprint, pencils or charcoal to each student.
5. Ask one student to pose, showing action. Students will quickly sketch the pose. Time the pose anywhere from 30 to 60 seconds.
6. After the student has done two or three poses, choose another student, and repeat step 5.
7. Repeat steps 5 and 6 several times, using five to six different students.
8. Challenge the students by asking two to three students to pose at the same time. Students hold the pose for one to two minutes, and through three different poses.
9. Repeat step 8 several times.

## Contour and Blind-Contour Drawing

Contour drawing forces the viewing of object outlines and are not sketches. It is a tool to improve observational skills.

1. Students retrieve the drawing techniques worksheet and pencils.
   [Once the term is drawn and defined, return worksheet to the Inside Art Binder.]
2. Define contour and blind contour drawing.
3. Gather several objects together and demonstrate a contour drawing using one continuous line, observing the objects and the paper.
4. Pass out newsprint and pencils to each student.
5. Arrange some simple objects together for all to see.
6. Give students five minutes to draw their first contour.
7. Rearrange objects and repeat step 6.
8. Repeat step 7, but allow students to only look at the objects, not their paper.
9. Compare and discuss the techniques and results of both.
10. Arrange a group of more complex objects, or ask a student to pose.
11. Give students about ten minutes to draw their contour.
12. Repeat steps 10 and 11 as time allows.

## Shading of Objects

Shading is the next step in rendering and drawing objects. Shading shows the representation of light.

1. Demonstrate shading of simple objects - cones, spheres and cubes.
2. Pass out newsprint and charcoal to each students.
3. Students practice drawing and shading the same objects of step 1.
4. Arrange objects [fruit, bottles, bowls] on draped fabric with a direct light source. Room lights should be dimmed.
5. Direct students to first draw the contours, and then represent the light and shadows by shading the objects. Students should represent the objects by rendering what they see.
6. Repeat steps 4 and 5 several times, changing the objects and lighting direction.

## One- and Two-Point Perspective

1. Students retrieve the drawing techniques worksheet and pencils.
   [Once the term is drawn and defined, return worksheet to the Inside Art Binder.]
2. Define and demonstrate one- and two-point perspective.
3. Pass out 11x17 blank paper, pencils and rulers.
4. Take students outside and face a building so that they only see one side.
5. Instruct students to draw a point on the far edge of the paper. They use this as their vanishing point.
6. Students draw the side of the building with all its details [windows, moldings, doors, signage].
7. Collect one-point drawings and pass out 11x17 blank paper.
8. Students move to the corner of the building so that they see two sides at once.
9. Students draw a vanishing point on both edges of the paper and draw both sides of the building with all details.
10. Display and discuss one- and two-point perspectives.

## Introduction to Hatching - Albrecht Dürer

This brief lesson introduces hatching and cross-hatching techniques. Albrecht Dürer used these techniques in his precise and detailed art. Proceed directly to the next lesson after introducing and discussing Dürer.

1. Pass out Albrecht Dürer handout, read and discuss.
2. View and discuss Dürer's art, defining and observing hatching and cross-hatching.

# Area Guide - Drawing

## Hatching and Cross-Hatching

During this lesson and the one following, students work on a small scale. These lessons are to practice the techniques before working on the final composition.

1. Students retrieve the drawing techniques worksheet and pencils.
   [Once the term is drawn and defined, return worksheet to the Inside Art Binder.]
2. Demonstrate hatching and cross-hatching using simple geometric shapes - cone, sphere and cube.
3. Pass out newsprint and pencils to each student.
4. Students practice hatching and cross-hatching on the same objects of step 2.
5. Give each student a black and white printout of an animal. Students will use these as reference to draw an animal using hatching and cross-hatching techniques.
6. Pass out 6x9 inch white paper and black ink pens to each student.
7. Students first lightly sketch the animal in pencil before using ink.
8. Display works and save animal printouts for the stipple lesson.

## Stipple

Stippling is a time consuming process. Be sure to give enough class time for students to complete their works.

1. Students retrieve the drawing techniques worksheet and pencils.
   [Once the term is drawn and defined, return worksheet to the Inside Art Binder.]
2. Show examples of stipple art.
3. Pass out animal printouts from the hatching lesson, 6x9 inch white paper, pencils and black ink pens to each student. Each student using the same animal.
4. Students first sketch the animal lightly in pencil before rendering it using uniform dots of ink.
5. Display works with the hatched animal drawings and discuss.

## Final Composition

The final composition is an animal drawing, but more involved and larger than the previous lessons. Students use both the hatching and stippling techniques to create the final work.

1. Pass out 9x12 or 12x15 inch white paper, pencils and black ink pens to each student.
2. Give each student one animal photo, which is a different image from the previous lessons and is more complex.
3. Explain the project to the students. They should lightly sketch their drawing first, then use a combination of hatching and stippling to produce their work. They need to show details and render the images to the best of their abilities.
4. Display final compositions.

# DRAWING TECHNIQUES

Name _____

Define and draw each drawing techniques.

CONTOUR DRAWING

BLIND-CONTOUR DRAWING

GESTURE DRAWING

HATCH

CROSS-HATCH

STIPPLE

ONE-POINT PERSPECTIVE

TWO-POINT PERSPECTIVE

# Leonardo da Vinci
[1452-1519] Italy

Leonardo da Vinci was born near Florence and trained as a painter and sculpture in the studio of Andrea del Verrocchio. Perhaps because the art scene was less competitive in Milan, he moved there around 1481. To get work, Leonardo advertised his abilities in architecture, water works, military engineering, sculpture and painting.

While in Milan, Leonardo worked to unify and balance life's conflicting experiences in his paintings. He believed that modeling with light and shadow and the expression of emotional states was very important in paintings. He also wanted to discover the underlying laws in nature and its processes.

"The Last Supper" is known as Leonardo's most impressive work. Painted on a wall in the Church of Santa Maria delle Grazie in Milan between 1495 and 1498, "The Last Supper" shows dramatic movement and the focus on Christ. He is isolated and framed by the window in back and the perspective is focused on him.

The "Mona Lisa" is Leonardo's most famous portrait paintings. It was his favorite as well, and he never parted from it.

Due to his perfectionism, curiosity and experimentalism, Leonardo produced few paintings. He did, however, sketch almost 2,500 drawings ranging from quick ink sketches to red and black chalk finished drawings. His studies for his paintings and sculptures included many poses and gestures.

In addition to being known as a painter, Leonardo was also well-known as an architect and sculptor. His notebooks include many central-plan building drawings and drawings of monumental equestrian statues. But no buildings have been attributed to Leonardo, and no sculptures have survived much past his time.

Later in his life, Leonardo was interested in science. He often said that his scientific work was done to help make him a better artist. Leonardo's precise drawings of cutaways and exploded views originated the method of scientific illustrations. He studied the human figure and anatomy as well as zoology, botany and geology.

After one of his equestrian statues was destroyed by the French occupying Milan in 1499, Leonardo, outraged by his work's destruction, moved to Florence. Around 1500, Leonardo returned to Milan as an artist under the service of the French. Leonardo later lived in Rome and finally in France, at the invitation of King Francis I, where he died in 1519.

# ALBRECHT DÜRER [ALL-brekt DYURE-ur]
## [1471-1528] Germany

Albrecht Dürer was born in Nuremberg, Germany, and was a brilliant painter and printmaker. Before being trained as a painter and engraver, he apprenticed for his father, a goldsmith.

Dürer was fascinated by Italian theories of art of his time and traveled to Italy twice to experience and learn more about the Italian Renaissance art movement. He thought that the Italians found secrets to creating beauty in art. Dürer was the first Northern artist to study Italian Renaissance art.

Dürer made it his mission to bring the modern [Italian] style to the North. He believed that the art in the North was crude in comparison. Good art also had rules, according to Dürer, and there is right and wrong in art.

He was the first celebrity artist outside of Italy, and in fact was know as the "Leonardo of the North" [Leonardo da Vinci]. Due to his tremendous fame, he became friends with some of German society's most prominent figures.

In his own time, Dürer was best known as an engraver. With his great abilities in woodcutting and engraving, he illustrated for books and sold prints of his work. He became known as the "people's artist" since ordinary people could buy his work. As a result, Dürer sold many prints which made him a very wealthy man.

Many of his prints were terrifying views of the Apocalypse or the Revelations of St. John. They were depictions in graphic detail of doomsday and its preceding omens. The prints were technical achievements in light and shading of the time. Dürer's work is still known for its advanced technical precision and detail.

In his later work, Dürer illustrated nature. He believed that art should be firmly fixed in nature, and it holds beauty, which lies in ordinary nature.

Throughout his life, Dürer was outspoken about art of the day, how it should be improved and what his ideals were. He was influential to artists and the graphic arts of his time as well as today.

| PERIOD | STUDENT NAME | TOTAL POINTS | GRADE |

**LESSON POINTS** _____ [165]

**ATTENDANCE POINTS** 30 - ____ = ____
TOTAL MINUS DEDUCTIONS

| LESSON | PARTICIPATION | COMPLETION | QUALITY | TOTAL POINTS |
|---|---|---|---|---|
| Gesture Drawing | 1 2 3 4 5 | 1 2 3 4 5 | 1 2 3 4 5 | |
| Contour and Blind-Contour Drawing | 1 2 3 4 5 | 1 2 3 4 5 | 1 2 3 4 5 | |
| Shading of Objects | 1 2 3 4 5 | 1 2 3 4 5 | 1 2 3 4 5 | |
| One- & Two-Point Perspective | 1 2 3 4 5 | 1 2 3 4 5 | 1 2 3 4 5 | |
| Hatching and Cross-Hatching | 2 4 6 8 10 | 2 4 6 8 10 | 2 4 6 8 10 | |
| Stipple | 2 4 6 8 10 | 2 4 6 8 10 | 2 4 6 8 10 | |
| Final Composition | 3 6 9 12 15 | 3 6 9 12 15 | 3 6 9 12 15 | |

Participation: was the student a part of discussions, worked throughout class. Completion: student's work - did they follow directions, finish assignments. Quality: is the work carefully created, well thought-out, show self-expression.

**Attendance** Daily recording, marking late or absent and workspace/materials cleaned and stored. L=late. A=absent. ✓=clean workspace.

8/21 / A / ✓

**ATTENDANCE DEDUCTIONS**

#of Late = ____ x ____ = ____   #of Absent = ____   #of Dirty space = ____   Total = ____

**195 TOTAL POINTS**

| A = 195-182 | C+ = 155-151 |
| A- = 181-176 | C = 150-143 |
| | C- = 142-137 |
| B+ = 175-170 | D+ = 136-131 |
| B = 169-162 | D = 130-123 |
| B- = 161-156 | D- = 122-117 |

Drawing — Grading Rubric — VISUAL ART for the secondary grades

# 2D aRT 1: ReaLiSM, IMPReSSiONiSM aND POST iMPReSSiONiSM

Introduction . . . . . . . . . . . . . . . . . . . . . . . . . . . . . . . . . . . . . . . . . . . . . . page 38

Area Guide - Realism . . . . . . . . . . . . . . . . . . . . . . . . . . . . . . . . . . . . . . page 38

Realism Artists

    Francisco de Goya . . . . . . . . . . . . . . . . . . . . . . . . . . . . . . . . . . . . . page 40

    John James Audubon . . . . . . . . . . . . . . . . . . . . . . . . . . . . . . . . . . page 41

Area Guide - Impressionism . . . . . . . . . . . . . . . . . . . . . . . . . . . . . . . page 42

Impressionism Artists

    Édouard Manet . . . . . . . . . . . . . . . . . . . . . . . . . . . . . . . . . . . . . . . page 45

    Claude Monet . . . . . . . . . . . . . . . . . . . . . . . . . . . . . . . . . . . . . . . . page 46

    Edgar Degas . . . . . . . . . . . . . . . . . . . . . . . . . . . . . . . . . . . . . . . . . page 47

Area Guide - Post-Impressionism . . . . . . . . . . . . . . . . . . . . . . . . . . . page 48

Post-Impressionism Artists

    Georges Seurat . . . . . . . . . . . . . . . . . . . . . . . . . . . . . . . . . . . . . . . page 50

    Paul Cézanne . . . . . . . . . . . . . . . . . . . . . . . . . . . . . . . . . . . . . . . . page 51

    Vincent van Gogh . . . . . . . . . . . . . . . . . . . . . . . . . . . . . . . . . . . . . page 52

    Paul Gauguin . . . . . . . . . . . . . . . . . . . . . . . . . . . . . . . . . . . . . . . . page 53

Grading Rubric . . . . . . . . . . . . . . . . . . . . . . . . . . . . . . . . . . . . . . . . . . page 54

Area Guide - Realism | page 38 | VISUAL ART for the secondary grades

## INTRODUCTION TO 2D ART 1.
This area covers the Realism, Impressionism and Post Impressionism movements. These movements include important artists that influenced future generations of artists and their work. They should be taught in order presented here. The lessons of this area are also divided by the movements.

## REALISM OBJECTIVES.
Students will explore and discuss the Realism movement. Students will learn about Francisco de Goya and John James Audubon, including their lives and their art. Students will create a realistic view of a botanical specimen from their local area.

## REALISM OVERVIEW.
Artists during this movement tried to create optical reality in art. They used real events and ordinary, everyday people for their art. The camera and the art of photography were invented during this time. Photography and painting sometimes clashed, although both strove to represent truth and the real in art.

## SUPPLIES NEEDED.
12x15 inch white paper, colored pencils, drawing pencils, Francisco de Goya and John James Audubon handouts, examples of their work (available at www.svisualart.com), movement/art worksheet (page 120), Inside Art Binder.

## MEDIA USED.
Colored pencils

## REALISM LESSONS.

### About the Artists - Goya and Audubon

1. Introduce and discuss the Realism movement, pass out movement/art worksheet and pencils.
2. Pass out Francisco de Goya handout, read and discuss.
3. View and discuss Goya's art.
4. How did Goya impact his viewers then and now? Has our view of his work changed over time? How and why?
5. Pass out John James Audubon handout, read and discuss.
6. View and discuss Audubon's art.
7. Compare these two Realist artists. What are their similarities? Differences? With work so different, why are they both Realists?

### Botanical Specimens

In this lesson, students create a realistic work of a botanical specimen from their local area. Gather specimens of plants, trees and flowers local to your area, or images of the specimens, or ask students to bring a specimen.

1. Go over Realism and its goal. [depict real life while representing its truth]
2. Explain the project to the students. They will be using colored pencils to depict a specimen, which they will show the details of that specimen.
3. Demonstrate the basics of using colored pencils - shading, blending, etc.
4. Give each student a specimen, 12x15 white paper, colored pencils, and a drawing pencil.
5. Students lightly draw then color their specimen, and they should also label the specimen.
6. Display the finished works.

# Francisco de Goya [Frahn-SEESE-coe de GOE-yah]
[1746-1828] Spain

A prolific artist, Francisco de Goya is known as the most important and independent Spanish artist and as a fairly good amateur bullfighter. He was appointed painter to Charles III in 1774 at the age of 28 and then to Charles IV in 1789. Goya was part of the royal workshops throughout most of his life and through four ruling monarchies.

He was intimately associated with the aristocratic world of Madrid, through which he received many commissions for portraits. He chose not to paint the noble world though, or flatter his subjects. Goya's portraits of royals and aristocrats were without illusion, but with unflattering and unflinching truths. It is believed that his subjects lacked the intelligence to recognize the true meanings in his portraits.

One of his best known works, "Charles IV of Spain and His Family", depicts the royals as pathetic, mediocre, pompous freaks, dripping with jewels and clothed in silks and velvet. The family enjoyed the work without understanding Goya's true depiction of them. The painting was even nicknamed "the grocer and his family who have just won the big lottery". Goya added himself to the painting, working at his easel in the shadows.

Goya recorded the sickness of the world around him and the evils of his time. He lived in a violent world of wars, and witnessed the Napoleonic invasions of Spain from 1808 to 1814, guerrilla warfare, the famine of 1812, and the rape, slaughter and mutilation of war. Goya created paintings, etchings, drawings and frescos [on the walls of his homes] depicting specific events of war and the experiences of life. He showed faceless soldiers, bleak landscapes and subjects without heroes with emotional color.

Goya lost his hearing at the age of 46 in 1792. He could only visualize the world around him, and was an isolationist, observing life from seclusion. At the age of 56, his mistress died, and ten years later, in 1812, his wife of 36 years died as well. It is reported that he had 20 children with his wife, but only some of them lived.

After losing both his wife and mistress, Goya became more of an isolationist. In 1820, he left Madrid and went into seclusion in his country house, "La Quinta del Sordo" [Deaf Man's Villa]. Goya created his "black paintings" while living there. These works were midnight colored nightmares depicting horrors, human bestiality and nightmarish creatures of the absurd.

Goya left Spain in 1824 and voluntarily exiled himself in Bordeaux, France. His eyesight started failing and he began to work in lithography. He produced four large works before his death in 1828 at the age of 82.

# JOHN JAMES AUDUBON
[1785-1851] Haiti

John James Audubon was born to French and Creole parents in 1785, in Saint Domingue [now called Haiti], but was raised by his stepmother in France, where he studied painting. At the age of 18, in 1803, Audubon was sent to America. It is believed he left France in part to escape serving in Napoleon's army.

Living near Philadelphia, he began as a portrait painter. In his free time he hunted, studied and drew birds. He married Lucy Bakewell and conducted the first known bird-banding experiment in North America.

Audubon and his wife eventually traveled to western Kentucky, where he opened a dry-goods store. He continued to draw birds as a hobby, and he often collected his specimens and brought them back to his studio to paint or draw. He had a bit of misfortune in 1819, as he was briefly jailed for bankruptcy. Soon after his release, he left Lucy in Kentucky and floated down the Mississippi River with a gun, art supplies and an assistant.

In 1826, Audubon sailed to England with his partially completed collection of bird paintings and drawings. He became an overnight success, found a printer for his collection and collaborated with an ornithologist to produce life histories of each bird species. The collection was known as the "Birds of America" and 435 life-size prints of birds were included in four volumes that were produced between 1827 and 1838. They were simple compositions of scientific accuracy, painted in watercolors and pastels. Each print included the species habitat and Audubon represented the living qualities of his subjects.

He made several trips back to America to search for birds and animals, and eventually moved to New York. Senility took over in his last years, and he died at the age of 65 in 1851.

Area Guide - Impressionism
page 42
VISUAL ART
for the secondary grades

### IMPRESSIONISM OBJECTIVES.
Students will explore and discuss the Impressionist movement. Students will learn about Éduoard Manet, Claude Monet and Edgar Degas, including their lives and their art. Students will examine the effects of light on landscapes and paint a landscape representing various lights and using an Impressionistic style.

### IMPRESSIONISM OVERVIEW.
Artists took the ideas of depicting the ordinary subjects of Realism a step further. Impressionists wanted to represent color and light. They believed in recording the appearance of the physical world and the changing of colors with the changing light. They also concluded that shadows were not composed of gray or black, but composed of color.

### SUPPLIES NEEDED.
Soft pastels, thick 12x15 inch textured paper, watercolors, 12x15 inch or larger watercolor paper, brushes, water, palettes, drawing pencils, camera, color photographs of landscapes, Éduoard Manet, Claude Monet and Edgar Degas handouts, examples of their work (available at www.svisualart.com), movement/art worksheet (page 120), Inside Art Binder.

### MEDIA USED.
Soft pastels
Watercolors

# IMPRESSIONISM LESSONS.

## About the Artists - Manet, Monet and Degas

1. Introduce and discuss the Impressionist movement and pass out movement/art worksheet and pencils.
2. Pass out Édouard Manet handout, read and discuss.
3. View and discuss Manet's art.
4. Pass out Claude Monet handout, read and discuss.
5. View and discuss Monet's art.
6. Pass out Edgar Degas handout, read and discuss.
7. View and discuss Degas' art.
8. Compare the works of Manet and Monet, are their styles different or similar? How do they compare to the works of Degas? How are they different than the works of the Realist artists?

## Landscapes in the Light

This lesson has two versions, classwide and individual. Both study the effects of light and color, and both can be used for this lesson. [Both are included on the grading rubric.] In the classwide version students all paint the same landscape, from the same view, just from different days, times, sunny, cloudy days, or seasons. Working from photographs are the best solution for this, [but it requires more preparation], and need to show many different lights, much like the work of Monet. The individual version requires less preparation, with each student painting three versions of the same landscape.

CLASSWIDE:

1. Find a landscape scene that you can return to over a period of time. Take photographs from the same position in the early morning, midday, evening, sunset, on sunny, overcast and cloudy days, and if time, during different seasons. Make sure there are enough images for your class, so each student has a different photo to work from.
2. Give each student a different color image to draw and paint their landscapes.
3. Explain the project to the students. They will paint their landscape in the colors of the photograph, depicting the particular light of day represented in the photograph. Light and color are the most important elements to depict, the objects of the landscape are secondary.
4. Demonstrate how to use soft pastels.
5. Pass out 12x15 inch or larger textured paper, soft pastels and drawing pencils.
6. Students lightly sketch the landscape before coloring, and a label of the time and/or day should be included.
7. Display the works together. Discuss the differences in color over the various paintings and how light affects color.

# Area Guide - Impressionism

INDIVIDUAL:

1. Instruct students to find a landscape they like and can easily go to. Have them use a camera to take three photographs of that location - in the morning, midday and evening. The three photographs can be taken on different days, and in different weather conditions.
2. Print out color images of student photographs.
3. Explain the project to the students. They will paint their landscape three times, in the colors of each photo, showing brushstrokes much like the Impressionist painters, and emphasizing the depiction of light and color.
4. Pass out 12x15 inch watercolor paper, watercolors, brushes, water and drawing pencils.
5. Students lightly sketch the landscape before painting.
6. Display the finished works, grouping all three together. Ask other students to guess the time of day represented in the works. Discuss the affects of light on color.

# ÉDOUARD MANET [Aid-ooh-AHR Mah-NAY]
[1832-1883] France

Édouard Manet hoped to be a naval officer, but gave up after failing the entrance exam twice. He went to Paris as a teenager to become an artist. Manet first painted as a Realist, but began the Impressionist movement.

Every year in Paris there were juried exhibitions called the Academy Salons. Rejection from the Salons often resulted in future failure. Acceptance or winning prizes resulted usually in professional success. At the age of 29, in 1861, Manet was awarded an honorable mention for one of his works. In 1863, he had his work rejected. In fact, more than one half of the works submitted that year were rejected. Due to the public outcry following all the rejections, Napoleon III formed the Salon des Refusés [Salon of the Rejected].

Manet displayed his work, "Luncheon on the Grass", at the Salon des Refusés, and it shocked the public. The figures were based on living, known people, his favorite model, his brother and a sculptor friend. The men were wearing 1860's Parisian attire, but the woman was naked. She looked at ease being naked, even looking at the viewer. Manet's work outraged the public, in part due to the immorality of the subject. If the men and women were nymphs who were naked or in Classical dress, the public would have accepted the work.

Manet began to lighten his colors and increase his brushstrokes in his paintings. He believed form was a function of paint and light and he studied the effects of light on figures and objects. Manet strove to show the arrested moment, and optical effects of light, but not while telling a story. No longer using flat patches of color, he forced the viewer to look at the painted surface. He began the shift in painting from the real to the abstract.

Manet was never accepted by his critics and suffered deeply because of their hostility towards him. He never understood their animosity, but continued to seek their approval. Upset over his critics, Manet traveled to Spain in 1865. But there he was further disappointed, he had thought Spain would be more picturesque and colorful.

Rejected by the Salon again in 1866 and 1867, Manet decided to display his own works. He used his inheritance to build a pavilion where he exhibited 50 of his works.

Although Manet had troubles with his critics, he was on good terms with many of his artist peers. At first he had a strained relationship with Claude Monet. Not only were their names similar and sometimes confused, but also Manet thought Monet was copying his style. Eventually the two became close, and Manet even supported Monet financially for a time.

His health began to deteriorate towards the end of his life. Manet continued to paint until his death in 1873. Almost immediately, his critics began to think his work was great and his paintings began to sell.

# Claude Monet [Klohd Moan-AY]
[1840-1926] France

Claude Monet was the son of a grocer. His parents refused to support his career as an artist. By sixteen, however, he was known already as a caricaturist in his hometown. Monet moved to Paris at the age of 22 to really begin his art career. There he lived in poverty, begging from friends, and often without money for paints. His young wife died of malnutrition. Up to 1888, Édouard Manet supported Monet financially.

In his work, he tried to forget the objects and reduce all of the visual experiences to terms of pure light. At first he painted people he knew, but he had no real interest in painting humans. Monet often said he wished he was born blind so he could then gain sight, not knowing what the objects were he was painting.

He was fascinated by the effects of light and its relationship with color. Monet even invented the name, "instantaneity", to describe what he was trying to accomplish. He painted the same place over and over again, creating series of works. He painted his favorite locations at differing times of day, morning, midday and evening, and then on bright days, gray days and during the different seasons. Monet painted 40 views of the Rouen Cathedral, 16 views of the Waterloo Bridge in London and 15 views of haystacks.

He is often credited with beginning the Impressionist movement. Monet's rejection from the Salon des Refusés in 1874 led him and several others to produce their own exhibition. They held successful exhibitions of their works, and called themselves Impressionists, although the term was first used disparagingly to describe one of Monet's works.

At the age of 50, in 1890, Monet finally was prosperous. He spent his later years at Giverney, painting a series of his water-garden there. Monet died wealthy and well-respected in 1926 at the age of 86.

# EDGAR DEGAS [Day-GAH]
## [1834-1917] France

Edgar Degas was an aristocrat whose father was a banker. A natural draftsman, his talents were encouraged by his father. To be less aristocratic, he changed his name from "de Gas" to Degas in 1870.

He lived with a detachment to the world around him, and although he is considered to be an Impressionist, Degas called himself "independent". He was the only Impressionist interested in depicting individuals, often painting personalities he knew. Degas was also not interested in the outdoor landscapes of the Impressionists. His outdoors were the city streets or the race track. He said he needed the artificial life and light, painting scenes of the indoors, the theater or cafes. He painted from his sketches and notes, and thought his work was the most spontaneous of the Impressionists, snapshots of the world around him.

Degas showed his works in the Impressionist exhibitions, although they didn't really like him, but they needed his money. After visiting his family in New Orleans, he annoyed the other Impressionist members by spouting ideas no one else wanted. Many saw Degas as a snob, and it is said that he showed his worst in public and reserved his affection for only a few, none of which were his peers. He was wealthy and refused to sell any of his work. He would only give it away.

Degas started painting ballet pictures after the mid 1870s. The ballet was indoors and full of unexpected shapes and artificial light. He liked the contrast of the glamour of the ballet with the plain girls dancing.

After 1875, he abandoned working in oils. He didn't like the texture of oils. Degas only worked in pastels, drawing and painting all at once.

After 1886, Degas became more detached from the world around him. He saw few people, exhibited rarely, and became a recluse in his studio. He soon had to sell his work. His wealth was gone from bailing out his brother in 1876 from difficulties with American stocks.

His sight also failed. Forms in his work became diffused. He began creating more sculptures. Degas could feel with his hands what his eyes could not see. He suffered bouts of depression, but continued to work as late as 1912. He died at the age of 83 in 1917.

# Area Guide - Post Impressionism

## POST IMPRESSIONISM OBJECTIVES.
Students will explore and discuss the Post Impressionist movement. Students will learn about Georges Seurat, Paul Cézanne, Vincent van Gogh and Paul Gauguin, including their lives and their art. Students will use dots of color to create a work of pointillism. Students will use texture and thick paint strokes in a complementary color painting.

## POST IMPRESSIONISM OVERVIEW.
The Post Impressionists took a more systematic approach to creating art than the Impressionists. They depicted everyday subjects, but focused on the three-dimensional space, line, pattern and color. Artists used arbitrary, vivid color, deliberately distorted color and unexpected combinations of color. Brushstrokes were distinctive and thick paint application was often used.

## SUPPLIES NEEDED.
Fine or ultra fine paint markers [or fine-tipped markers], thick 9x12 inch smooth paper, acrylic paints, brushes, gel medium, canvas, boards or acrylic paper, water, palettes, drawing pencils, Seurat, Cézanne, van Gogh and Gauguin handouts, examples of their work (available at www.svisualart.com), movement/art worksheet (page 120), Inside Art Binder.

## MEDIA USED.
Paint markers
Acrylic paints

## POST IMPRESSIONISM LESSONS.

### About the Artists - Seurat, Cézanne, van Gogh and Gauguin

1. Introduce and discuss the Post Impressionist movement and pass out movement/art worksheet and pencils.
2. Pass out Georges Seurat handout, read and discuss.
3. View and discuss Seurat's art.
4. Pass out Paul Cézanne handout, read and discuss.
5. View and discuss Cézanne's art.
6. Pass out Vincent van Gogh handout, read and discuss.
7. View and discuss van Gogh's art.
8. Pass out Paul Gauguin handout, read and discuss.
9. View and discuss Gauguin's art.

10. Compare the works of the Post Impressionists to the Impressionists. What makes the works so different? What are the main characteristics of the Post Impressionists' work? How is Vincent van Gogh's work different than Georges Seurat's work? What principles of art do they both use? Is one principle more dominant? How did Vincent van Gogh express mood in his works?

## Dots of Color

1. Arrange several objects [vase, flowers, fruit, vegetables] on a draped table.
2. Review pointillism, its characteristics and demonstrate how to use the paint markers.
3. Explain the project to the students. They will create a pointillist picture, using paint markers and depict the shape, shadow and color of the objects. They will use random and overlapping dots of color.
4. Pass out 9x12 inch paper, pencils and paint markers.
5. Students lightly draw the objects and shadows before applying dots.
6. Display and discuss student works.

## Deliberate Complements

1. Ask students to take a picture of their bedroom, taken from the doorway of the room.
2. Review Vincent van Gogh's works, especially the "Bedroom in Arles" picture.
3. Print images in black and white. They don't need to be color as the colors used will not be actual colors.
4. Explain the project to the students. They will depict their room using thick paint strokes and complementary colors. Other colors can be used, but mainly the complements.
5. Write complementary pairs onto small pieces of paper, creating enough for each student to get one.
6. Randomly pass out complement pairs, and canvas, pencils, brushes and acrylics.
7. Students lightly draw their room and the objects in it.
8. Students paint their rooms using the complementary colors.
9. Display and discuss student works. Compare to Vincent van Gogh's room.

# Georges Seurat [JEE-orge Suh-RAH]
[1859-1891] France

Georges Seurat was born in Paris to a wealthy family. Little is known about his life. He never talked about his short life, he was always a very private person.

Bothered by the disintegrating forms of the Impressionist painters, Seurat sought to redefine boundaries of forms and solidify masses. He is known to be the most systematic painter throughout history. He simplified forms into basic geometrical shapes and controlled the content of his paintings by integrating those forms into space.

Seurat brought a scientific view to painting, calculating a precise arrangement of color. He studied books on color theory and optics and investigated the golden section. He developed a method of applying primary and secondary colors directly to the painting surface, allowing the viewer's eyes to optically mix the colors into the proper of final color of the form.

His color application is similar to that of modern printing. Seurat's method is known as pointillism, applying color in precise dots, and divisionism, using individual strokes of color. This was difficult and painstaking work that made the process time consuming.

One of his most famous paintings, "Sunday Afternoon on the Island of La Grande Jatte" took Seurat over two years to paint. He first made a long series of studies of the Jatte and the people in it. The painting is not a snapshot in time, but an assembling of figures of geometric shapes, made of tiny dots of color. The painting is also very large, six feet nine inches high by ten feet wide, with 67 square feet of canvas.

Seurat contracted pneumonia in 1891, and died at the age of just 32. He was working on developing and experimenting with more complex shapes and compositions. His work called "The Circus" was never finished. Seurat didn't sell nor give away many paintings during his short life, but he was a large influence to many artists. Most artists throughout time have practiced pointillism and studied his painting technique.

# Paul Cézanne [Say-ZAHn]
[1839-1906] France

Paul Cézanne studied painting in Paris and began painting in 1860. He was an influential artist who believed Impressionism lacked form and structure. He aimed not for truth in appearance, but the structure behind color, and to bring an intellectual order to the presentation of color.

Cézanne used the landscapes around his home as his subjects. He would study his subjects, which he called his "motifs", and their color for long periods of time. Light, time of day and atmospherical effects on his motifs were not important. He painted outdoors in order to absorb the essence of the landscape.

He was the opposite of Seurat's precise and scientific approach to painting. Every stroke was an experiment and he didn't know if the next stroke would make or ruin his paintings. He still studied the elements of art and the relationships of objects to each other.

He explored the properties of line, plane and color, defining his motifs into planes of color. The planes were sharp, defined solids approaching geometric shapes. Through his planes, Cézanne sought to portray the actual visual experience of his motifs, instead of a fixed experience from one or two point perspective.

Cézanne hated working indoors or from sketches or memory. He often painted in seclusion and was a solitary man. He was friends with his contemporaries, and during the last decade of his life, he became well-known. Always painting outdoors, Cézanne was caught in a sudden storm in 1906. He collapsed and died soon after, at the age of 67.

# Vincent van Gogh [Vahn Go]
[1853-1890] Holland

Vincent van Gogh is described as a socially awkward, small and ugly, intense man. By his own choosing, he dressed badly and was said to be without charm or wit. He seemed incapable of enjoying himself or others around him, often irritating family and others. He wanted to be accepted and to please, but was resentful and angry at any criticism.

Van Gogh grew up in a family where the men usually became members of the clergy. Two uncles, however, operated an art gallery. At the age of 16, van Gogh went to work for his uncles, but after irritating so many customers, he was fired. He then turned to religion, but flunked out of the theological seminary. With his religious background, he thought he could be a social worker, trying to work with people in the mining districts and the slums of London. He was not successful at this either.

Finally in 1880, at 27 years old, he decided to become a painter. He had no formal training, but looked at it as having a spiritual calling. Van Gogh didn't attempt to earn a living with his art, he was more concerned with just painting. His work from 1880 through 1886 was drawn in crayon or charcoal with colors in greenish blacks and dismal browns, which were just as depressing as his subjects of the poor streets and farms, miners and peasants.

In 1886, van Gogh left for Paris where he was supported by his brother, Theo, who owned a gallery there. With the help of Theo, he was a student at the studio of Fernand Cormon, a conventional painter. At his studio, van Gogh again irritated everyone and was known as the class freak.

In Paris, van Gogh was persuaded to abandon his gloomy colors, and he started seeing the outdoors in vibrant and vivid colors. He developed his technique of painting in short, choppy strokes if bright color, his favorite being yellow. He used thick layers of paint and thick, heavy brushstrokes, sometimes even squeezing paint onto the canvas directly from the tube. He created a tactile experience to his paintings. Van Gogh explored complementary colors and the power if expressive lines.

When painting, van Gogh was obsessive. He'd work late into the night, without stopping to eat. He had several fainting spells from working too hard.

He thought Paris was dreary and that he was an annoyance and in the way to Theo. In 1888, at the age of 35, he left Paris for Arles in the south of France. Theo gave him money still, and helped him throughout his time in Arles. While there, van Gogh suffered epileptic seizures and hallucinations.

Van Gogh was a huge fan of Paul Gauguin, and convinced him to visit Arles. The two artists were in an incident, involving a violent quarrel. Afterwards van Gogh cut-off his ear, wrapped it up and then delivered it to a girl at a brothel he and Gauguin had visited.

Van Gogh remained in Arles through the first part of 1889. He was then an inmate at the asylum at Saint-Rémy for a year. There he painted 150 pictures, including "The Starry Night".

With no more seizures, he went back north to Auvers, near Paris, in 1890. He painted constantly, but still felt he was a burden to his brother. In fact, van Gogh created around 900 paintings and 1,100 works on paper during his life.

While in a wheat field, van Gogh began a letter to Theo, but stopped to perhaps paint. It is not known why or where he got a gun, but he shot himself below the heart. Somehow he was able to walk from the wheat field back to the inn he was staying at. Van Gogh remained lucid for two days before dying in the arms of his brother. He was just 37 years old.

# Paul Gauguin [Go-GEHn]
[1848-1903] France

As a child, Paul Gauguin and his parents moved to Peru. On the voyage over, his father died of a heart attack. He lived on his great uncle's estate in Lima until he moved back to France with his mother in 1855. At the age of 17, Gauguin became a merchant marine and he loved the primitive nature he saw in Martinque and Brittany.

As an adult, Gauguin was described as a brutally handsome, self-confident man. He was also known to be vain and selfish, and loved to be flattered. At the age of 23 he was a successful stock broker and bank agent until he lost that job in 1882. During this time, Gauguin painted and drew to relax.

Gauguin had a painting accepted to the Salons in 1876 at the age of 28. He bought paintings by Manet, Monet, Renoir, Cézanne and others of the time. He also started exhibiting with the Impressionists in 1879. Encouraged, Gauguin started painting as his career in 1883. He tried to support himself through painting and selling his work, and expected success would happen quickly, but ended up living off of odd jobs that barely paid his bills. His wife and children returned to her family in Denmark.

He grew restless for exotic places and searched for exotic forms for his work. Vincent van Gogh's brother, Theo, offered to pay for Gauguin to go to Arles to visit and help Vincent in 1888. There Gauguin found everything to be pretty, but became bored and restless. He only enjoyed the arguments over art he had with van Gogh, and only stayed because Theo was paying. He left Arles after about a year, and just three days after van Gogh cut-off his own ear after a violent argument they had.

In 1891, he went to Tahiti in search of the exotic. He lived in a simple wooden hut, married a young native girl, learned the language and myths of the culture, and painted naked all day. Gauguin used new and unexpected color combinations of rich, tropical colors and flattened forms to paint dark-skinned figures in native clothes, bananas, palms and flowering plants. He didn't paint reality, however, he painted combinations of western and European elements with the native people and nature of Tahiti.

He went back to France from 1893 to 1895 to collect money due to him and exhibit his work. While there, his uncle died, leaving him an inheritance. He met a woman, Anna, who became his companion, and they spent the money quickly. Anna abandoned him and ransacked his Paris studio after he broke his ankle in a fight.

Gauguin went back to Tahiti where he grew old quickly. He started spitting up blood, developed a rash, had open sores and lesions that wouldn't heal. He ran out of money, begged for money, even from his wife in Denmark. Gauguin lived off of boiled rice, then dry bread and water, and finally mangos he found. He attempted suicide by swallowing arsenic, but lived. He wrote nasty letters to government officials, and because of one, was sentenced to three months in jail. While appealing, he suffered two small strokes. With sight failing, he left Tahiti in 1901 for Marquesas, where he died alone in 1903.

| PERIOD | STUDENT NAME | | TOTAL POINTS | GRADE |
|---|---|---|---|---|
| | | | | |

| LESSON POINTS | QUIZ POINTS | ATTENDANCE POINTS |
|---|---|---|
| _____ [150] | _____ [30] | 30 - _____ = _____ <br> TOTAL MINUS DEDUCTIONS |

| LESSON | PARTICIPATION | COMPLETION | QUALITY | TOTAL POINTS |
|---|---|---|---|---|
| Botanical Specimen | 2 4 6 8 10 | 2 4 6 8 10 | 2 4 6 8 10 | _____ |
| Landscapes in the Light <br>   Classwide | 2 4 6 8 10 | 2 4 6 8 10 | 2 4 6 8 10 | _____ |
|   Individual | 2 4 6 8 10 | 2 4 6 8 10 | 2 4 6 8 10 | _____ |
| Dots of Color | 2 4 6 8 10 | 2 4 6 8 10 | 2 4 6 8 10 | _____ |
| Deliberate Complements | 2 4 6 8 10 | 2 4 6 8 10 | 2 4 6 8 10 | _____ |

Participation: was the student a part of discussions, worked throughout class. Completion: student's work - did they follow directions, finish assignments. Quality: is the work carefully created, well thought-out, show self-expression.

## Attendance
Daily recording, marking late or absent and workspace/materials cleaned and stored. L=late. A=absent. ✓=clean workspace.

| 8/21 |
|---|
| A |
| ✓ |

### ATTENDANCE DEDUCTIONS

#of Late = ____ x ____ = ____    #of Absent = ____    #of Dirty space = ____    Total = ____

### 180 TOTAL POINTS

| | |
|---|---|
| A  = 180-168 | C+ = 143-139 |
| A- = 167-162 | C  = 138-132 |
| | C- = 131-126 |
| B+ = 161-157 | D+ = 125-121 |
| B  = 156-150 | D  = 120-114 |
| B- = 149-144 | D- = 113-108 |

2D Art 1     Grading Rubric     page 54     VISUAL ART for the secondary grades

# 2D aRT 2: FauvisM, CUBisM and SURReaLisM

Introduction .................................................. page 56

Area Guide - Fauvism ........................................... page 56

Fauvism Artists

    André Derain ............................................. page 58

    Henri Matisse ............................................ page 59

Area Guide - Cubism ............................................ page 60

Cubism Artists

    Pablo Picasso ............................................ page 62

    Georges Braque ........................................... page 63

Area Guide - Surrealism ........................................ page 64

Surrealism Artists

    Salvador Dalí ............................................ page 67

    Frida Kahlo .............................................. page 68

    René Magritte ............................................ page 69

Grading Rubric ................................................. page 70

Area Guide - Fauvism
page 56
VISUAL ART
for the secondary grades

## INTRODUCTION TO 2D ART 2.
This area covers the Fauvism, Cubism and Surrealism movements. These movements further break away from Realism and work towards the abstract. They should be taught in order presented here, and are divided by the movements.

## FAUVISM OBJECTIVES.
Students will explore and discuss the Fauvists. Students will learn about André Derain and Henri Matisse, including their lives and their art. Students will use clashing, vibrant color to create a distorted landscape.

## FAUVISM OVERVIEW.
Artists were heavily influenced by the art of non-European cultures, and inspired by Vincent van Gogh and Paul Gauguin. Due to their use of simplified design and shockingly brilliant color, they were called Fauves, or wild beasts. Their art composed of sweeping brush strokes, showed intense, non-natural color, clashing primary colors, rich textures and energetic patterns.

## SUPPLIES NEEDED.
Acrylic paints, brushes, gel medium, canvas, board or acrylic paper, drawing pencils, water, palettes, André Derain and Henri Matisse handouts, examples of their work (available at www.svisualart.com), movement/art worksheet (page 120), Inside Art Binder.

## MEDIA USED.
Acrylic paints

## FAUVISM LESSONS.

### About the Artists - Derain and Matisse

1. Introduce and discuss the Fauvists and pass out movement/art worksheet and pencils.
2. Pass out André Derain handout, read and discuss.
3. View and discuss Derain's art.
4. Pass out Henri Matisse handout, read and discuss.
5. View and discuss Matisse's art.
6. Compare the works of Derain and Matisse. How are their works similar or different to the Post Impressionists? Is their work more distorted than the Impressionists? How? What elements do they use to express mood?

### Distortion with Color

1. Find images of bridges for students to reference and print out in color.
2. Review the Fauvist characteristics.
   [vivid, clashing color, non-naturalistic color, patterns of brush strokes]
3. Explain the project to the students. They will create a bridge landscape using the Fauvist characteristics. They should use colors not natural to the scene [like André Derain] and thick brush strokes.
4. Pass out acrylics, palettes, brushes, modeling paste, canvas, board or acrylic paper, bridge images and drawing pencils.
5. Students lightly draw the landscape before painting.
6. Display and discuss student works.

# ANDRÉ DERAIN [on-DRAY Dare-EHn]
[1880-1954] France

André Derain studied engineering until 1889, when he decided to become a painter. He attended the Académie Carriére, painted on the banks of the Seine, was influenced by Paul Cézanne and moved by Vincent van Gogh's paintings.

In 1901, Derain was commissioned into the army for three years, painting only while on leave. He left the army in 1904 and by 1905 was painting in London and the south of France with Henri Matisse. He was close friends with artists of his time and painted in various locations through the 1920s, moving from new studio to new studio.

Derain rejected the harmonies of Impressionism. He modified the traditional styles of the past by adding modern characteristics. He believed in making the strongest possible visual presentation. Derain distorted perspective, used strong linear patterns and non-naturalist bold colors, often clashing yellows, oranges, greens, reds and blues against black accents.

He was known to be a good painter, but some critics called him a parasite to art. Others believed him to be an innovator and a unique painter. Derain was a successful painter, becoming financially stable between 1910 and 1912, when an art dealer bought his entire collection of art and he was signed to an exclusive contract.

In the 1930s, Derain did many studies in forms of paintings, drawings, lithographs and etchings and in the early 1940s, produced a series of nearly 400 woodcuts. He also produced small clay sculptures of masks and figures that weren't discovered until after his death.

His vision never recovered fully after an eye infection he contracted a year before he died. Derain died in 1954, when he was hit by a moving vehicle in France.

# HENRI MATISSE [on-REE Ma-TEES]
[1869-1954] France

Henri Matisse persuaded his father to let him abandon studying law for a career in art at the age of 22. He first was a designer of tapestries and textiles before moving to Paris to study in 1891. In Paris, Matisse copied works from the Louvre, to study and to make money to survive. He began exhibiting his paintings in 1895, but felt he was still a student. He was influenced by other artists, and finally found new meanings in color in 1905.

Matisse created clashing strokes of pure, vibrant color, setting up movement through the colors. He found that color had its own structure and rhythms and could be entirely independent of the actual color of objects. He worked to maximize the intensity of color and believed that backgrounds could become just areas of color. He was also concerned with the formal organization of elements.

A group of artists surrounded Matisse, and in 1905 this resulted in the start of the Fauvist movement. But by 1907 the group started going in different, individual directions.

Around 1917, Matisse traveled to Nice in the south of France, where he lived for the rest of his life. His work became more relaxed and spontaneous. He produced his most informal work with paint applied casually and subjects more at ease and pleasurable.

In 1929, he traveled to America where he was commissioned to paint a large mural. He finished in 1933 and traveled through America and then to Tahiti before returning to France.

He did printmaking throughout his career, first working in copper in 1903 and then composing lithographs in 1906. In the 1930s, Matisse developed his work into more graphic pieces with two-dimensional patterns. His later years were spent producing a series of works cutting and pasting flat, brightly shaped papers.

In the late 1940s, when Matisse was almost 80 years old, he volunteered, [and partially paid for], to decorate an entire chapel near Nice. He did everything, from the stained-glass windows, murals, tiles, alter and crucifix, to even the doors, and anything else in the church. Matisse was never devout, and it was done in part because of his friendship with a nun.

During his lifetime, he produced many paintings, drawings, sculpture, etchings, linocuts, lithocuts, aquatints, paper cutouts and book illustrations. His subjects were landscapes, still life, portraits, interiors and female figures. Matisse died in 1954, at the age of 84.

# Area Guide - Cubism

## CUBISM OBJECTIVES.
Students will explore and discuss the Cubist movement. Students will learn about Pablo Picasso and Georges Braque, including their lives and their art. Students will use various textured and colored papers to create a collage still-life of musical instruments. Students will create self-portraits using the Cubist style of multiple planes of color.

## CUBISM OVERVIEW.
Cubists searched for new ways to depict form. Some used simple forms to represent nature. Others tried to make different angles of objects all at once. Geometric surfaces created were from formal elements from conception, not reality.

## SUPPLIES NEEDED.
Five to seven musical instruments, various textured and colored papers, canvas or hardboard, scissors, blank paper, glue, colored pencils, drawing pencils, acrylic paints, water, palettes, Pablo Picasso and Georges Braque handouts, examples of their work (available at www.svisualart.com), movement/artist worksheet (page 120), Inside Art Binder.

## MEDIA USED.
Collage
Acrylic paints

## CUBISM LESSONS.

### About the Artists - Picasso and Braque

1. Introduce and discuss the Cubist movement and pass out movement/art worksheet and pencils.
2. Pass out Pablo Picasso handout, read and discuss.
3. View and discuss Picasso's art.
4. Pass out Georges Braque handout, read and discuss.
5. View and discuss Braque's art.
6. Compare the works of Pable Picasso and Georges Braque. What are the main characteristics of their work? How does their use of media effect their style?

### Musical Collage

1. Gather several musical instruments and various papers of different textures and colors.
2. Arrange instruments creating a still life scene.
3. Explain the project to the students. They will create a collage painting of the instruments using various papers to form the shapes of the instruments. Papers should overlap and form individual planes. They can use paints or colored pencils to add detail.
4. Pass out blank paper and drawing pencils.
5. Students draw their still life before creating their collage.
6. Pass out papers, canvas or hardboard, glue and scissors.
7. Students cut and glue papers forming the instruments, and add detail with paints or colored pencils.
8. Display and discuss student works.

### Plane Portraits

1. Take portrait photographs of each student and print out in color.
2. Review Cubist portraits and their characteristics.
3. Explain the project to the students. They will paint self-portraits using multiple planes of color and with angular movement and fractured shapes. These are not realistic portraits.
4. Pass out portrait photographs, blank paper, canvas, pencils and acrylics.
5. Students sketch the portraits before lightly drawing them on canvas.
6. Students paint their portraits.
7. Display and discuss student works.

# Pablo Picasso [PA-bloh Pee-KaH-so]
[1881-1973] Spain

Pablo Picasso was an artistic genius who by the age of 12 was already a competent draftsman. In his youth, he mastered many historical styles and experimented with a wide range of visual expression. At 19, Picasso left Spain for Paris. Between 1901 and 1905, he painted in only two manners, which became known as his "Blue Period" and "Rose Period". Picasso painted in only variations of blue and then red. During his Blue Period, he painted worn, pathetic characters in harsh blues and greens, showing poverty, misery and a pessimistic mood. During his Rose Period, his mood changed with his colors. He painted vivid and charming reds, depicting flowers, performers and graceful figures.

In late 1906, Picasso discovered African sculpture and combined it with the style of Cézanne and the refinements of European painting. His graceful figures started changing to geometric forms and solids. He took Cézanne's planes of color further with bolder, fractured shapes and harsh, angular movement. He created ambiguous planes, suggesting combinations of views. Picasso became obsessed with finding a new way to represent forms.

In his early years of painting, he only showed his work to other painters. Before World War I broke out, he worked with fellow artist, Georges Braque. The two collaborated on many works, sometimes not knowing who created what.

In 1912, Picasso started creating collages, blending objects with paint on the canvas. He said he wanted to bring bits of the real world into the artificial. He also tried working in sculpture, bringing his angular planes to three-dimensional space.

In the 1920s, Picasso became inspired by the Italian classical world. He painted mythological images with mythical creatures like fauns, nymphs, centaurs and minotaurs. But in the 1930s, he changed his motifs again. He started using bold and harmonious color and gentle curves to paint expressive portraits of women. By 1936, Picasso became distraught over the Spanish Civil War, [he was still living in France], and painted anti-war paintings in protest.

From the late 1940s through the 1960s, Picasso painted, made ceramics and experimented with printmaking. He also gained international fame, exhibiting in London, Paris, Venice, Tokyo, Rome, Milan and New York. He painted into his 80s and 90s, amassing a personal fortune, and collecting work of other artists. Picasso died in 1973, at the age of 91.

# GEORGES BRAQUE [Joerj Brahk]
[1887-1963] France

Georges Braque was the son of a painting contractor who gave him his first art lessons. He studied at the School of Fine Arts in LeHavre, and then moved to Paris. He was influenced by other artists and African, Egyptian, and Greek sculpture.

Braque first depicted compositions of bowls of fruit, tables, goblets, compotes and musical instruments. Working closely with Pablo Picasso, he used various textured papers and commonplace colors to create his paintings.

He was concerned with the surface texture in his work and would add sand or other matter to his paints to add thickness and texture. He worked to create a controlled, harmonious method, and represent a multitude of planes with multiple points of view. Braque used muted, non-pure color, geometric patterns and large, intersecting planes.

During World War I, Braque was commissioned to serve in the French army. In 1915, he became temporarily blind from a head injury he received in the war. He couldn't paint again until 1917.

When Braque started painting again after the war, and he began using a brighter color palette. In the 1920s, he began including human figures, usually female nudes, into his compositions. He died at the age of 81 in Paris.

Area Guide - Surrealism

### SURREALISM OBJECTIVES.
Students will explore and discuss the Surrealist movement. Students will learn about Salvador Dalí, Frida Kahlo and René Magritte, including their lives and their art. Students will create two dream-like paintings, one on a flat surface and the other on a glass bottle.

### SURREALISM OVERVIEW.
Surrealists sought to portray the world of dreams, fantasy and the unconscious mind. They depict everyday objects into a dreamlike reality, bringing the outer and inner realities together.

### SUPPLIES NEEDED.
Acrylic paints, tempera or watercolors, canvas, board or paper, brushes, palettes, water, drawing pencils, empty glass bottles, lined paper, blank white paper, Salvador Dalí, Frida Kahlo and René Magritte handouts, examples of their work (available at www.svisualart.com), movement/art worksheet (page 120), Inside Art Binder.

### MEDIA USED.
Acrylic paints
Tempera or watercolors

## SURREALISM LESSONS.

### Random Things

Do not mention Surrealism before or during this lesson! Students will compose two lists of random items that they will later use to create their dreamscapes and painted bottles.

1. Pass out lined paper cut in half length-wise, with each student receiving two sheets, and pencils.
2. Ask students to write down the first things they think of. They need to form two lists when answering the following: [each list on a separate sheet of paper]
   a. List two different wild animals [no pets].
   b. List two different locations [i.e. - beach, city, ocean, island, mountains].
   c. List the weather on your last birthday and on the other sheet, list today's weather.
   d. List two everyday, non-electric objects [i.e. - backpack, pencil, book, pillow, stuffed animal].
   e. List two hand-held objects [i.e. - cell phone, calculator, mp3 player, camera, book].
   f. List two different fruits.
   g. List your favorite and least favorite color [not black, white or brown].
      List their complements on the other sheet.
   h. List two things you could sit on [i.e. - chair, log, pillow, bed, sofa, bench].
   i. In front of the hand-held objects on both sheets, write one of these adjectives:
      melted, shattered, stretched, disintegrated, crushed, pinched, smudged, torn, bloated, inverted, cracked, elongated, eroded.
3. Collect papers and save for later lessons.

### About the Artists - Dalí, Kahlo and Magritte

1. Introduce and discuss the Surrealist movement and pass out movement/art worksheet and pencils.
2. Pass out Salvador Dalí handout, read and discuss.
3. View and discuss Dalí's art.
4. Pass out Frida Kahlo handout, read and discuss.
5. View and discuss Kahlo's art.
6. Pass out René Magritte handout, read and discuss.
7. View and discuss Magritte's art.
8. Compare the works of Dalí and Magritte, two similar artists. What themes do they both use? Did Dalí create realism in his work? How does his choice of media effect the meaning? How is their work different from Kahlo?

## Dreamscapes

1. Review the characteristics of Surreal art.
2. Return one Random Things list to each student.
3. Explain the project to the students. They will use their list to create a Surreal painting. Each item should be included in the location and with the weather listed. Items don't need to be actual size and the hand-held objected should be depicted with the adjective describing it [i.e. - melted calculator]. They can add a person or themselves to the painting, and can use acrylics, watercolors or tempera.
4. Students lightly draw their picture before painting.
5. Students choose media to create their work.
6. Pass out supplies needed.
7. After finishing, students write a short description of their work.
8. Display works and descriptions and discuss.

## Painted Bottles

1. Collect empty glass bottles. Clean, rinse and remove their labels.
2. Prime bottles with white glass paint.
3. Review René Magritte's painted bottles, observing their characteristics.
4. Explain the project to the students. They will create their own Surreal bottle using their second Random Things list. They should include everything on their list, just like the previous lesson. They will use acrylics to paint their bottles.
5. Pass out bottles, their second Random Things list, scratch paper and pencils.
6. Students first sketch a rough composition on the scratch paper before drawing on the bottle.
7. Students paint the scene on their bottle. [Apply a sealant if necessary.]
8. Display bottles.

# Salvador Dalí [Sahl-vah-DORE Dah-LEE]
## [1904-1989] Spain

The son of an atheist and a Roman Catholic, Salvador Dalí was named in memory of a recently deceased brother, and often called himself a double, a replay of his brother. Dalí was an arrogant man with a flamboyant personality.

In 1921, he entered the Real Academia de Bellas Artes de San Fernando in Madrid. There he experimented in many styles. Dalí ended up being expelled for inciting a student rebellion and leaving an examination because he felt the instructors weren't qualified to judge him or his art.

Dalí moved towards Surrealism in 1928, exploring his own psyche and dreams in paintings, jewelry, sculpture, furniture and films. He invented his "paranoiac-critical method" to assist in his creative process. His goal was to destabilize the world, painting double and different images within one group of shapes, combining irrationality and imagination with the external world. To make his paintings as real as natural landscapes, Dalí rendered his dreamscapes with precise detail and control. In 1929, he made a film aimed to disorientate the viewer.

Dalí spent World War II living in the United States. He painted portraits, created a dream sequence for an Alfred Hitchcock film and planned a cartoon with Walt Disney.

He returned to Spain in 1948. Dalí created no more Surrealist art. Instead, he did paintings and drawings dealing with history, science and religion, but still used doubles as a subject.

The Teatre-Museu Dalí was founded in 1974. Dalí showed his work, shared his ideas and gave drawing classes there. After his death in 1989, he was buried at the Teatre-Museu.

# Frida Kahlo [FREE-duh KAH-low]
## [1907-1954] Mexico

Frida Kahlo is the most autobiographical of the Surrealist painters and also one of the most influential and important Mexican artists. She didn't plan to be an artist. After surviving polio as a child, she entered a pre-med program in Mexico City.

Kahlo began painting after a horrible bus accident in 1925. She was only 18, and she fractured her spine, ribs and collarbone, and was in constant pain afterwards. She also was not able to have children, and underwent 32 operations in her lifetime.

She painted, drew and sketched about 200 works during her life. Most were self-portraits in which she painted her pain and passion, and tried to separate herself from her pain. When asked why she painted herself so much, she'd say it was because she was the subject she knew best. Kahlo was also inspired by Mexican art and folk art, especially the colors and depictions of fantasy, violence and death.

At the age of 22, Kahlo married muralist, Diego Rivera, who was 20 years older than her. They both believed in Communism and were active members of the Communist Party in Mexico. They shared a passionate relationship filled of infidelities, including her bisexual affairs, a divorce, and a remarriage.

Only three exhibitions of her work were held in her lifetime. Her health deteriorated rapidly and in 1953, her right leg was amputated at the knee. Kahlo turned to alcohol and drugs. She died in 1954 at the age of just 47.

Kahlo said that when she died, she wanted her body burned, not put in the ground. It is said that the many mourners gathered in her memory at the crematorium witnessed a shocking event. Apparently, a blast of heat from the incinerator caused her body to lift up, showing through the open incinerator doors. Her hair was in flames, looking like a halo, and she seemed to smile as the doors closed. Kahlo's ashes were placed in the "Blue House" where she and Rivera lived. After his death, it opened as the "Museo Frida Kahlo".

# René Magritte
[1898-1967] Belgium

René Magritte was a painter, printmaker, draftsman, sculptor, photographer and filmmaker. When he was just 12 years old, his mother committed suicide in the Sambre River. It is said that he and his two brothers found her body with her nightgown up over her face. He was very private, and never talked about his mother's death.

Magritte studied at the Académie des Beaux-Arts in Brussels between 1916 and 1918. He first painted in the Impressionist style and then tried many different styles until 1926, when he created Surrealist paintings and signed a contract with a gallery. In 1926, he also played an important role in founding the Belgian Surrealist group.

He worked to disrupt conventions, alter forms and create new objects. Magritte wanted to redefine the images to words relationships and to have the viewer experience his works beyond their surface appearance. He hated the notion of one-of-a-kind art and often repeated his subjects and objects in new situations in different paintings. Magritte also created his standardized humans, mainly his man in a bowler hat. He incorporated words and texts into his paintings and took from literature, films and movies when titling his work.

During World War II until the 1960s, Magritte tried to show the beauty of life. He became internationally famous in 1948. In 1956, he produced a series of short, comical Surrealist films. Also during this time, he consciously mocked Impressionism and attacked the superficially of the French public.

Throughout his life, Magritte created more than 1,200 paintings. He also produced 67 wax sculptures based on his paintings. He died in his own bed at the age of 69, in 1967.

| PERIOD | STUDENT NAME | | TOTAL POINTS | GRADE |
|---|---|---|---|---|
| | | | | |

**LESSON POINTS**
_____ [150]

**ATTENDANCE POINTS**
30 - ____ = _____
TOTAL MINUS DEDUCTIONS

| LESSON | PARTICIPATION | COMPLETION | QUALITY | TOTAL POINTS |
|---|---|---|---|---|
| Distortion with Color | 2 4 6 8 10 | 2 4 6 8 10 | 2 4 6 8 10 | _____ |
| Musical Collage | 2 4 6 8 10 | 2 4 6 8 10 | 2 4 6 8 10 | _____ |
| Plane Portraits | 2 4 6 8 10 | 2 4 6 8 10 | 2 4 6 8 10 | _____ |
| Dreamscapes | 2 4 6 8 10 | 2 4 6 8 10 | 2 4 6 8 10 | _____ |
| Painted Bottles | 2 4 6 8 10 | 2 4 6 8 10 | 2 4 6 8 10 | _____ |

Participation: was the student a part of discussions, worked throughout class. Completion: student's work - did they follow directions, finish assignments. Quality: is the work carefully created, well thought-out, show self-expression.

## Attendance
Daily recording, marking late or absent and workspace/materials cleaned and stored. L=late. A=absent. ✓=clean workspace.

| 8/21 |
| A |
| ✓ |

**ATTENDANCE DEDUCTIONS**
#of Late = ____ x ____ = ____   #of Absent = ____   #of Dirty space = ____   Total = ____

**180 TOTAL POINTS**

| | |
|---|---|
| A = 180-168 | C+ = 143-139 |
| A- = 167-162 | C = 138-132 |
| | C- = 131-126 |
| B+ = 161-157 | D+ = 125-121 |
| B = 156-150 | D = 120-114 |
| B- = 149-144 | D- = 113-108 |

2D Art 2 — Grading Rubric — page 70 — VISUAL ART for the secondary grades

# 2D aRT 3: CONTEMPORARY aRT and POP aRT

Introduction . . . . . . . . . . . . . . . . . . . . . . . . . . . . . . . . . . . . . . . . . . . . . page 72

Area Guide - Contemporary Art . . . . . . . . . . . . . . . . . . . . . . . . . . . . . . . page 72

Contemporary Artists

    Mark Rothko . . . . . . . . . . . . . . . . . . . . . . . . . . . . . . . . . . . . . . . . page 74

    Jackson Pollock . . . . . . . . . . . . . . . . . . . . . . . . . . . . . . . . . . . . . page 74

Area Guide - Pop Art . . . . . . . . . . . . . . . . . . . . . . . . . . . . . . . . . . . . . page 75

Pop Artists

    Andy Warhol . . . . . . . . . . . . . . . . . . . . . . . . . . . . . . . . . . . . . . . page 78

    Jasper Johns . . . . . . . . . . . . . . . . . . . . . . . . . . . . . . . . . . . . . . . page 79

Grading Rubric . . . . . . . . . . . . . . . . . . . . . . . . . . . . . . . . . . . . . . . . page 80

Area Guide - Contemporary Art

## INTRODUCTION TO 2D ART 3.
This area covers the Contemporary Art and Pop Art movements. In these movements, abstract art creation takes hold.

## CONTEMPORARY ART OBJECTIVES.
Students will explore and discuss Contemporary Art. Students will learn about Mark Rothko and Jackson Pollock, including their lives and their art. Students will combine the styles of the two artists into one piece. Students will create an abstract work depicting patterns, shapes and movement.

## CONTEMPORARY ART OVERVIEW.
The changing world after World War II brought new ideas in design and a wide array of new styles. Formal approaches to art conflicted with conceptional approaches to art. Artists sought to change the perceptions and behaviors of the viewer. Abstract Expressionists wanted to make human contact and reawaken inter connectedness with all living things through art filled with spontaneous energy. Color-field painters believed they could create whole environments with organic forms and fields of color. The Formal Abstractionists used pure form, mathematical shapes and geometric patterns to express the new technological age they were living in.

## SUPPLIES NEEDED.
Canvas, acrylic paints, brushes, sticks, blank paper, drawing pencils, water, palettes, Mark Rothko and Jackson Pollock handouts, examples of their work (available at www.svisualart.com), movement/art worksheet (page 120), Inside Art Binder.

## MEDIA USED.
Acrylic paints

## CONTEMPORARY ART LESSONS.

### About the Artists - Rothko and Pollock

1. Introduce and discuss Contemporary art and pass out movement/art worksheet and pencils.
2. Pass out Mark Rothko handout, read and discuss.
3. View and discuss Rothko's art.
4. Pass out Jackson Pollock handout, read and discuss.
5. View and discuss Pollock's art.
6. What are the characteristics of contemporary art? Are the works of Rothko and Pollock innovative? Why? What moods are created with their works?

### Color Field Drips

1. Write colors on small pieces of paper, making enough for each student to get one color, and pass out. [12 different colors: red, red-orange, red-purple, orange, yellow, yellow-orange, yellow-green, green, blue, blue-green, blue-purple, purple]
2. Explain the first part of the project to the students. They will use their color to create a color field painting. The background should be a shade of their color. The largest area, their color, and two other areas, tints, tones or close variations of their color.
3. Pass out canvas, acrylic paints and brushes.
4. Students paint their color fields.
5. After drying, explain the second part of the project. Students will drip paint onto their color fields, using the complementary color of their color field, white, black and gray. They will create patterns with the drips.
6. Either work outside or create an area on the floor, place canvases and students paint using sticks or other tools [not brushes].
7. Display and discuss student works. How do they compare to the works of Rothko and Pollock?

### Free Abstract

1. Review contemporary art characteristics.
2. Explain the project to the students. They will create an abstract work using geometric patterns and shapes, organic color fields and movement through texture and color. This piece does not need to be realistic.
3. Pass out blank paper, pencils, canvas and acrylics.
4. Students first plan their work, sketching ideas before painting.
5. Students paint their abstract work.
6. Display and discuss student works, students present their ideas.

# MARK ROTHKO
[1903-1970] Russia

Mark Rothko is the best known color-field painter. Born in Russia, he grew up in the United States after emigrating with his family in 1913. From 1921 to 1923, he studied liberal arts at Yale University. After Yale, Rothko moved to New York where he attended only a few art classes. He was basically a self-taught artist, learning by attending exhibitions of other artists and visiting artist studios.

Rothko's early works up to the late 1920s were muddy toned landscapes, still-life and bathers. By the 1930s, his work showed a sense of eerie moods, mystery and dread with tragic figures in unnatural colors. In the 1940s, Rothko's work changed again. He started using symbols and emotions of ancient myths, trying to communicated them as directly as possible.

By the mid 1940s, he started using abstract, organic forms. Gradually he reduced his forms from human figures to compositions of two to three rectangles of color. Rothko said he didn't remove the human figure, he just replaced it with shapes. His compositions featured subtle tonal variations of intense color and hazy contours with soft edges. He explored monochromatic effects of color, and he preferred to have his work exhibited far from the work of other artists.

Late in his life, Rothko became depressed, and it showed in his works. He was drinking and smoking heavily, didn't exercise and ate a poor, unhealthy diet even though he was diagnosed with a heart defect. He committed suicide at the age of 66, when he slit his wrists and overdosed on anti-depressants.

# JACKSON POLLOCK [PAUL-ock]
[1912-1956] America

Jackson Pollock grew up in the southwestern United States, and in 1929 studied painting in New York. From 1938 to 1942, he worked for the Federal Art Project, which supported artists and provided art to hospitals and schools.

By the mid 1940s, Pollock was painting completely abstract art. He said he wanted to bring his memories of the landscapes of the West and the sand painting techniques of Native Americans to his paintings.

Using sticks, trowels and knives instead of brushes, Pollock poured and flung paint onto his canvas. He used his whole body and worked from all four sides of the canvas, which was rolled out on the floor. He liked to be able to walk around the canvas.

In Pollock's free, abstract style, he abandoned traditional composition. There were no easily identifiable shapes and no direct reference to nature, but there were rhythmic layers of lines of color.

Pollock's work and style were supported by many critics and viewers. But in 1956, Time Magazine called him "Jack the Dripper". He died in 1956, in a car crash. By the 1960s, he was recognized as an important figure to abstract art.

## Area Guide - Pop Art

### POP ART OBJECTIVES.
Students will explore and discuss Pop Art. Students will learn about Andy Warhol and Jasper Johns, including their lives and their art. Students will take mass-produced objects and create screen prints depicting those objects. Students will use letters and numbers to create works of art with encaustic paints.

### POP ART OVERVIEW.
Pop Art began after World War II with artists taking from popular culture. They took their subjects from the materialistic feel of American advertising, industrial design, Hollywood and comic books. They combined mass-media images and artifacts with traditional art techniques.

### SUPPLIES NEEDED.
Screens with frames, squeegees, drawing fluid, screen filler, black screen ink, canvas, acrylic paints, camera, photocopier, encaustic paints in red, yellow, blue, white and black, hot palettes, water, brushes, hot air gun, blank paper, hardboard or canvas coated with gesso, Andy Warhol and Jasper Johns handouts, examples of their work (available at www.svisualart.com), movement/art worksheet (page 120), Inside Art Binder.

### MEDIA USED.
Screen printing
Encaustic paints

# Area Guide - Pop Art

# POP ART LESSONS.

## About the Artists - Warhol and Johns

1. Introduce and discuss Pop Art and pass out movement/art worksheet and pencils.
2. Pass out Andy Warhol handout, read and discuss.
3. View and discuss Warhol's art.
4. Pass out Jasper Johns handout, read and discuss.
5. View and discuss John's art.
6. Discuss the characteristics of Pop Art. Why did the works of Warhol and Johns become so popular? How does their choice of media influence their work? What effect does the media have on their style? How did their work play a role in today's culture? How will today's technology effect the visual arts?

## Screened Objects

SCREEN PRINTING: Trace the image in REVERSE onto a screen. Use drawing fluid to paint only the image. When dry, paint around the image and the rest of the screen with screen filler. Wash off the drawing fluid when the screen filler is dry. Apply screen ink and squeegee [following product directions] onto canvas or paper.

1. Review the characteristics of Andy Warhol's art.
2. Ask students to bring a mass-produced object to class, and photograph each object.
3. Print images and photocopy them to produce a black and white image with no grays, just solid blacks and solid whites.
4. Demonstrate the screen printing process.
5. Explain the project to the students. They will divide a canvas or thick paper into six equal spaces. They will paint different color combinations into each space. They then screen print the object's image onto each space using black screen ink.
6. Students draw and then paint their reversed images onto their screens.
7. Between the steps to create their screen, students divide and paint their canvas.
8. Students paint the screen with the screen filler, and when dry, wash off the drawing fluid.
9. Allow students to practice printing on scratch paper before printing on their screens.
10. Display and discuss student works.

## Letters and Numbers

1. Demonstrate how to paint with encaustics and safety when using hot palattes and hot air gun.
2. Write one letter or number on small pieces of paper. Randomly pass out papers to the students. They will paint that letter or number.
3. Explain the project to the students. They will use only red, yellow, blue, white and black encaustic paints to layer and render their letter or number.
4. Pass out canvas, pencils and scratch paper.
5. Students first sketch their letter or number on paper, then lightly draw it on their canvas.
6. Using hot palettes and hot air guns, students layer paints, creating their paintings.
7. Display student works and discuss the process of encaustic painting.

# ANDY WARHOL [WAR-hall]
## [1928-1987] America

Andrew Warhola was born between 1928 and 1931. He said he was born in 1928 and that his 1930 birth certificate was a forgery. He studied at the Carnegie Institute of Technology from 1945 to 1949 and worked in a department store during the summers. In 1949, he legally shortened his name to Andy Warhol and moved to New York, where he worked as a commercial artist and illustrator for Harper's Bazaar and Vogue. His first solo exhibit was in 1952, but continued to support himself as a commercial artist until 1962.

Warhol's subjects were what he saw in the mass media, commercial design and advertising, and news photos of disasters, famous people and criminals. He used photo-screens to create his paintings as well as rubber stamps, silkscreens and stencils to draw shocking images. Warhol produced many series of many objects, including Campbell's soup cans, stamps, Coca-cola bottles, and Brillo pads. He also created art installations of sculptures based on mass produced items. He was fascinated with the idea of fame and its fragility. He believed that in the world of mass media, that everyone could become famous for 15 minutes.

Sometime between 1952 and 1955, he dyed his hair a straw color. In 1962, Warhol rented an attic that became his studio. He named it the "Factory". Most of his work was screenprints of photographic images on painted backgrounds of color. He had many young artists surrounding him at the Factory, and he called them the "workers". Between 1962 and 1964, the Factory produced over 2,000 pictures. Warhol would conceive the picture and his workers would do the rest.

He visited Paris in 1965 and announced he was quitting painting. He was only going to make experimental films, but he still painted limited edition prints. One film he produced, called "Empire", was in black and white and eight hours long.

In the 1970s, Warhol said he was transformed from a commercial artist into a business artist. He created commissioned portraits printed off of Polariods, and made a large amount of money. Now wealthy, he was able to indulge his compulsive shopping habits. He bought jewelry and art ranging from the decorative to Native American and American folk art. In the 1980s, Warhol returned to painting, producing work with religious themes.

He died in 1987, due to complications following gall-bladder surgery. Over 2,000 people attended his memorial service. In 1994, the Andy Warhol Museum opened in Pittsburgh.

# JASPER JOHNS
[1930- ] America

Named after revolutionary war hero, Sergeant William Jasper, Jasper Johns was raised in South Carolina. He studied art at the University of South Carolina between 1947 and 1948. At the urging of his art teachers, he moved to New York in late 1948 to apprentice as a commercial artist.

From 1951 to 1952, during the Korean War, he had to serve two years in the army and was stationed in South Carolina and Japan. Johns returned to New York in 1953, working at book stores and as a decorator.

In the mid 1950s, he started incorporating things the mind knows already, symbols from mass media, into his work. The generic symbols included targets, American flags, numbers, letters, ale cans and the United States map. Johns also worked on sculptures of flashlights, light bulbs and beer cans, and in the 1960s, he created assemblages and started integrating words into his paintings.

Johns used complex processes, working in encaustic and newspaper collage. Encaustic is an ancient method of using molten wax with pigment to paint. He would first cover a canvas with newspaper and then paint it with the quick-drying encaustic paints.

He lives and works in New York, and is known as one of the most significant and influential American painters of the twentieth century. In 1989, he was appointed as an honorary member of the Royal Academy of London. In 2011, Johns received the Presidential Medal of Freedom from President Barrack Obama.

His works are extremely rare to acquire, and his early paintings sold for around $1,000. In 1973, "Double White Map" sold for $240,000, and in 1980, "Three Flags" sold for $1 million. In 2006, "False Start" was bought for $80 million.

| PERIOD | STUDENT NAME | | TOTAL POINTS | GRADE |
|---|---|---|---|---|
| | | | | |

| LESSON POINTS | ATTENDANCE POINTS |
|---|---|
| _____ [120] | 30 - ____ = _____ <br> TOTAL MINUS DEDUCTIONS |

| LESSON | PARTICIPATION | COMPLETION | QUALITY | TOTAL POINTS |
|---|---|---|---|---|
| Color Field Drips | 2 4 6 8 10 | 2 4 6 8 10 | 2 4 6 8 10 | _____ |
| Free Abstract | 2 4 6 8 10 | 2 4 6 8 10 | 2 4 6 8 10 | _____ |
| Screened Objects | 2 4 6 8 10 | 2 4 6 8 10 | 2 4 6 8 10 | _____ |
| Letters and Numbers | 2 4 6 8 10 | 2 4 6 8 10 | 2 4 6 8 10 | _____ |

Participation: was the student a part of discussions, worked throughout class. Completion: student's work - did they follow directions, finish assignments. Quality: is the work carefully created, well thought-out, show self-expression.

## Attendance
Daily recording, marking late or absent and workspace/materials cleaned and stored. L=late. A=absent. ✓=clean workspace.

Key: 8/21 / A / ✓

### ATTENDANCE DEDUCTIONS
#of Late = ____ x ____ = ____  #of Absent = ____  #of Dirty space = ____  Total = ____

### 150 TOTAL POINTS

| | |
|---|---|
| A = 150-140 | C+ = 119-116 |
| A- = 139-135 | C = 115-110 |
| | C- = 109-105 |
| B+ = 134-131 | D+ = 104-101 |
| B = 130-125 | D = 100-95 |
| B- = 124-120 | D- = 94-90 |

2D Art 3 — Grading Rubric — page 80 — VISUAL ART for the secondary grades

# 2D aRT 4: pRiNTMaKiNg aNd pHOTOgRapHy

| | |
|---|---|
| Introduction | page 82 |
| Area Guide - Printmaking | page 82 |
| Printmaking Artists | |
|     Edvard Munch | page 84 |
| Area Guide - Photography | page 85 |
| Photographers | |
|     William Henry Fox Talbot | page 88 |
|     Ansel Adams | page 89 |
| Grading Rubric | page 90 |

# Area Guide - Printmaking

## INTRODUCTION TO 2D ART 4.
This area covers printmaking and black and white photography techniques. Three artists, Edvard Munch, William Henry Fox Talbot and Ansel Adams and their works are also discussed.

## PRINTMAKING OBJECTIVES.
Students will learn about Edvard Munch, including his life and his art. Students will create a linocut print by carving a linoleum block and impressing the image onto paper. Students will etch a scratchboard image.

## SUPPLIES NEEDED.
5x7 inch linoleum blocks, 6x6 inch scratchboard, white chalk, fixative, colored india inks, scratchboard tools, linoleum cutters, printing inks, brayers, paper for printing, color bird images (available at www.svisualart.com), blank paper, drawing pencils, Edvard Munch handout, examples of his work (available at www.svisualart.com).

## MEDIA USED.
Linocuts
Scratchboard

# PRINTMAKING LESSONS.

## About the Artist - Munch

1. Pass out Edvard Munch handout, movement/art worksheet and pencils, read and discuss.
2. View and discuss Munch's art.
3. Discuss the themes Edvard Munch used in his works. What techniques did he use in his woodcuts and lithographs?

## Linoshapes

1. Demonstrate linoleum carving, printing and safety.
2. Explain the project to the students. They will create a geometric shape and/or pattern surrounded by a border by carving and cutting linoleum. Once completed, they will use printing inks, their linoleum and paper to create a series of prints.
3. Pass out blank paper, pencils, linoleum and cutters.
4. Students first draw on paper then on the linoleum. The image will be the reverse of the printed piece.
5. Students carefully carve their linoleum, and once finished, students can rinse the linoleum.
6. Students apply printing inks to the linoleum and press to paper, repeating three to five times using different colors.
7. Display and discuss student works.

## Scratch Birds

1. Demonstrate scratchboard etching techniques and safety.
2. Pass out a color image of a bird to each student. Students will use these as a reference when etching and painting their scratchboards.
3. Explain the project to the students. They will etch a scratchboard image of their bird, then paint the white areas.
4. Pass out 6x6 scratchboard, blank paper, pencils, white chalk and scratchboard tools.
5. Students first draw the bird on paper, then use the chalk to draw the image on the scratchboard.
6. Students etch away the black, revealing white areas, depicting the textures and features of the bird.
7. Clean the scratchboard and fix with a fixative.
8. Students paint the colors of the bird in the white areas with india inks.
9. Fix again.
10. Display and discuss student works.

# EDVARD MUNCH [ED-varhd Moonk]
## [1863-1944] Norway

Edvard Munch was often sick as a child, and his family moved several times when he was very young. His father was a successful sea captain and timber merchant, then a doctor. His mother suffered from tuberculosis and died when he was young.

At the age of 12, Munch began drawing. The inside of his family home and its objects were his subjects. In 1879, he studied at the Kristiania Technical College. He decided to be a painter and in 1880, he registered at the Royal School of Design in Kristiania. He left a year later and rented a studio with other students. Munch first exhibited his work in 1883, and traveled abroad for the first time in 1889, to Paris.

Back in Kristiania, he arranged a one man exhibition, and then went back to Paris in late 1889 on a scholarship. While in Paris, his father died, and he fell into a period of melancholy and depression. He also experimented with different painting methods.

In his work, Munch was a critic of modern man. He believed that humans were powerless against death and love and tried to portray his beliefs in his art. He said that his ideas came spontaneously, and he would repeat his same disturbing visions in oil paintings, woodcuts and lithographs.

Munch exhibited in Berlin in 1882, and became famous as a result. His exhibition closed after just a week, due to an overwhelmingly bad reaction against his painting methods. He returned home to Kristiania and became friends with poets and philosophers and rented a studio.

He then spent his next years in Berlin, Paris, Prague and a resort in the Baltic, where he believed someone was spying on him. Munch was admitted to a clinic in Copenhagen, where he underwent various cures, including electric shock. He now saw Kristiania as the place where the enemy lived and vowed never to live there again. He rented a home on the coast, built an open air studio, and was inspired by the countryside and the people. But he then returned to Kristiania in 1916, settling west of the city. There he lived in isolation and traveled less.

He was almost blind for three years in 1930, after a blood vessel burst in his right eye. In the winter of 1943/44, he contracted pneumonia and died peacefully in his home.

# Visual Art for the secondary grades

## Area Guide - Photography

### PHOTOGRAPHY OBJECTIVES.
Students will explore and discuss various photography techniques. Students will learn about William Henry Fox Talbot and Ansel Adams, including their lives and their art. Students will reproduce the beginning techniques of photography by creating sun exposed prints. Student will develop, enlarge and print black and white photographs. Students will hand-color a black and white photograph.

### SUPPLIES NEEDED.
8x12 inch sun printing sheets, botanical specimens, a sunny day, cameras, dark room with developing equipment (or local commercial photo lab or digital camera that can take black and white images), photo paper, photo oils or pencils, William Henry Fox Talbot and Ansel Adams handouts, examples of their work, examples of hand-colored photographs (available at www.svisualart.com), movement/art worksheet (page 120), Inside Art Binder.

### MEDIA USED.
Sun prints
Photography
Hand-coloring

# PHOTOGRAPHY LESSONS.

## About the Artists - Talbot and Adams

1. Pass out William Henry Fox Talbot handout, movement/art worksheet and pencils, read and discuss.
2. View and discuss Talbot's art.
3. Pass out Ansel Adams handout.
4. View and discuss Adam's art.
5. How has each artist impacted photography? How does their work in photography effect their style? How does their use of photography influence meaning?

## Paper Prints

1. Collect botanical specimens. [i.e. ferns, branches, leaves, etc.]
2. Explain the project to the students. They will create sun exposed prints like the work of Talbot. They will each take a botanical specimen, place it on the sun print paper and expose it to the sun. They can place a second specimen on top of the first exposure, creating a double image.
3. Pass out specimens and take students outside.
4. Follow directions of the sun print paper for exposure time and stopping the exposure.
5. Display student work and discuss the process and what they've learned.

## Black and White Photography

If your classroom does not have a dark room, one can be created in a storage room or large closet. Install a red light and make sure that no light can entire the room. Students can develop film and contact prints, but will need an enlarger to create full size photographs. A local photo lab can develop the film also, or digital cameras can be used. Make sure the digital camera takes a black and white image. Do not take color photographs and convert them in a photo-manipulation program.

1. Demonstrate developing techniques.
2. Students take black and white photographs of nearby landscapes, scenery or buildings. These should not be snapshots, but rather thought out compositions [much like Ansel Adams] that frame and artfully depict the subject matter.
3. Develop film and create contact sheets.
4. Students choose three images they want to enlarge into 8x10 prints.
5. Develop prints.
6. Display and discuss student works.

## Colorized Black and Whites

Hand-coloring of black and white photographs began soon after the start of photography. This process was the easiest way to create color photography and was used through the 1950s. Some artists still hand-color black and white photographs.

1. View examples of hand-colored photographs.
2. Demonstrate hand-coloring techniques.
3. Explain the project to the students. They will choose one of their black and white prints, reprint and color. This print should have good details and textures and not large areas of solid black or white.
4. Give each student a small practice photograph and photo oils or pencils to color first.
5. Pass out student prints.
6. Students carefully color their black and white photograph.
7. Display both black and white version and colorized version. Discuss the hand-coloring process and its results.

# William Henry Fox Talbot
[1800-1877] England

Known as the "father of photography", William Henry Fox Talbot was an intelligent and shy man. He graduated from Trinity College in Cambridge and was an elected member of Parliament, but that is not where his passion lied. Talbot was curious in many fields, including mathematics, chemistry, astronomy, botany, art history and philosophy, and was fascinated by light. He was a scientist exploring the early world of photography, and published four books, over 50 scientific papers and held 12 English patents.

In 1834, after becoming frustrated with the camera obscura and camera lucida, Talbot started experimenting with getting an image to paper. His process involved coating fine writing paper with salt and a silver nitrate solution, which he then pressed a leaf or plant on, then topped with glass and left it in the sun. After darkening, Talbot coated the paper with salt again to stop the process. he was able to create precise tracings of botanical specimens, calling it "the art of photogenic drawing" [now called photograms]. These early works were not stable, and can not be exhibited because they would fade in even low light.

In 1839, Talbot presented his process to the Royal Society of England. He had heard that a Frenchman, Louis Deguerre, was getting ready to reveal his different process, and wanted his process presented first. Talbot continued to develop his process more and in 1841 patented his "calotype" process. A friend suggested using hypo-sulfite of soda, "hypo", to stop the development, a technique still used today for developing black and white photographs.

Talbot's early works were negative images. He soon learned that if he let light shine through the negative image onto another sheet of paper, the result would be a positive image. He created many prints using this method. Talbot's subjects were of plants, flowers, leaves, trees, still-life, sculpture and statuaries. During this time, between 1841 and 1846, Talbot took almost all the photogenic drawings he is know for.

Talbot made few prints after 1846, because he was more obsessed with perfecting his process. In fact, he spent his last 25 years developing and perfecting an effective photogravure [ink reproduction] process. Over 6,000 of his images are at the Science Museum in London.

Camera obscura - a darkened chamber or box, in which images of outside objects are projected onto a flat surface through an aperture or small hole.

Camera lucida - an optical instrument attached usually to a microscope, by which the outside object is projected on a flat surface.

# ANSEL ADAMS
[1902-1984] America

Ansel Adams was born in San Francisco into a wealthy family. When he was four years old, he fell and broke his nose, [which marked him for life], during an aftershock of the 1906 San Francisco earthquake. The family fortune collapsed in 1907.

Adams lived a solitary childhood and had problems fitting in at school. He was not successful at any of the schools his parents sent him to, and his father and aunt eventually tutored him at home. He found joy in nature, hiking around his home, and taught himself to play the piano and read music at the age of 12. Adams then took formal training and by 1920, he was a professional pianist.

From 1916 on, he started spending time in Yosemite, and joined the Sierra Club in 1919. Yosemite inspired him to photography and his first photographs and writings were published in the 1922 Sierra Club Bulletin. By the late 1920s, Adams realized he could survive off photography and had his first one man exhibition in 1928 at the Sierra Club's San Francisco headquarters. In 1934, he was elected to the Club's board of directors.

Adams used a large-plate view camera to record the natural grandeur of the scenery he saw. He created sharp focus through the use of the smallest lens aperture and never manipulated the image in the darkroom to alter its clarity. He would visualize the picture before taking each photograph, and each image was no accident. He believed that one should master the techniques of photography to be ready to capture the image.

He made lengthy trips to the Southwest and the American mountain wilderness. He remained busy, but was financially broke in 1935. Adams realized he had to be a commercial photographer to survive. His clients included the National Park Service, Kodak, IBM, AT&T, Life and Fortune Magazines.

He served as principle photographic consultant to Polariod, and produced ten volumes of technical photography manuals. Adams died of a heart attack in 1984, at the age of 82.

| PERIOD | STUDENT NAME | | TOTAL POINTS | GRADE |
|---|---|---|---|---|
| | | | | |

**LESSON POINTS**
_____ [135]

**ATTENDANCE POINTS**
30 - _____ = _____
TOTAL MINUS DEDUCTIONS

| LESSON | PARTICIPATION | COMPLETION | QUALITY | TOTAL POINTS |
|---|---|---|---|---|
| Linoshapes | 2 4 6 8 10 | 2 4 6 8 10 | 2 4 6 8 10 | _____ |
| Scratch Birds | 2 4 6 8 10 | 2 4 6 8 10 | 2 4 6 8 10 | _____ |
| Paper Prints | 1 2 3 4 5 | 1 2 3 4 5 | 1 2 3 4 5 | _____ |
| Black and White Landscapes | 2 4 6 8 10 | 2 4 6 8 10 | 2 4 6 8 10 | _____ |
| Colorized Black and Whites | 2 4 6 8 10 | 2 4 6 8 10 | 2 4 6 8 10 | _____ |

Participation: was the student a part of discussions, worked throughout class. Completion: student's work - did they follow directions, finish assignments. Quality: is the work carefully created, well thought-out, show self-expression.

## Attendance
Daily recording, marking late or absent and workspace/materials cleaned and stored. L=late. A=absent. ✓=clean workspace.

8/21
A
✓

**ATTENDANCE DEDUCTIONS**

#of Late =____ x ____ = ____   #of Absent =____   #of Dirty space =____   Total = ____

**165 TOTAL POINTS**

| | |
|---|---|
| A = 165-154 | C+ = 131-128 |
| A- = 153-149 | C = 127-121 |
| | C- = 120-116 |
| B+ = 148-144 | D+ = 115-111 |
| B = 143-137 | D = 110-104 |
| B- = 136-132 | D- = 103-99 |

2D Art 4   Grading Rubric   page 90   VISUAL ART for the secondary grades

# 3D Art 1: Pottery and Wood Carving

| | |
|---|---|
| Introduction | page 92 |
| Area Guide - Pottery | page 92 |
| Minoan Pottery | page 94 |
| Area Guide - Wood Carving | page 95 |
| Oceania Art | page 97 |
| Grading Rubric | page 98 |

Area Guide - Pottery

## INTRODUCTION TO 3D ART 1.
This area covers pottery and wood carving. If your classroom has access to a kiln and potter's wheel, students can throw thin pots and vases, and learn how glazes change when fired. If not available, use air drying clays and paint. Wood carving basics are reviewed and students work to create simple carvings.

## POTTERY OBJECTIVES.
Students will discuss and view Minoan pottery and sculptures. Students will form human figures using simple geometric shapes, and depict realistic animals. Students will create pots and/or vases painted with abstract patterns and motifs.

## SUPPLIES NEEDED.
Clay, water, table coverings, animal pictures, clay tools, glazes or paints, brushes, drawing pencils, blank paper, animal images, Minoan art handout, examples of their work (available at www.svisualart.com), movement/art worksheet (page 120), Inside Art Binder.

## MEDIA USED.
Clay and glazes

## POTTERY LESSONS.

### The Minoans
1. Pass out the Minoan Art handout and pass out movement/art worksheet and pencils.
2. Read and discuss.
3. View examples of their sculpture and pottery.
4. Compare their art to contemporary art. How are they similar? Different?

### Geometric Human Figures
1. Review Minoan figures and their characteristics.
2. Explain the project to the students. They will create their own figure using geometric shapes. The figure can be standing, sitting or showing an action.
3. Pass out blank paper and pencils.
4. Students sketch their figure before working with the clay.
5. Pass out clay, water and table coverings [to protect tables].
6. Students shape their figures.
7. Allow figures to dry, and then fire.
8. Display and discuss student works.

## Area Guide - Pottery

### Animals in 3D

1. Retrieve animal photos for students to use as a reference.
2. Demonstrate how to use sculpting tools.
3. Explain the project to the students. They will mold the clay into animals. They should try to depict the animal with as many details as possible. Animals should be about 10 inches or less in length. When sculpting the animal, it is best to start with geometric shapes.
4. Pass out clay, animal images, water, sculpting tools and table coverings.
5. Students mold and sculpt their animals.
6. Dry sculpted animals and fire.
7. Display and discuss student works.

### Coil Pots

1. Demonstrate how to create a simple coil pot or vase.
2. Pass out clay, water and table coverings.
3. Students roll the clay into thin ropes and then coil them into the form of a pot.
4. Students use water, clay tool or woodstick to help them smooth the sides of the pots, removing the coil lines.
5. Dry pots and paint with glazes and fire.

### Decorative Pots and Vases

1. Review Minoan pottery and their characteristics.
2. Explain the project to the students. They will create a coil pot or vase decorated with geometric patterns and animal shapes. They can form patterns with clay or use sculpting tools to create the outlines and use paint or glaze to color the patterns. [If the class has access to a potter's wheel, demonstrate and have students try to form pots that way.]
3. Pass out clay, water, clay tools and table coverings.
4. Students form their pot or vase and add decorative patterns and animals.
5. Allow to dry, paint and fire.
6. Display, discuss and compare student works to Minoan pottery.

# Minoan Art

During the Bronze Age, the Minoan Civilization, a peaceful and prosperous race, lived on the island of Crete. We know very little about their history. Their pottery shows us the greatest evidence of Minoan life.

At first, their pottery depicted abstract, spiral forms and scrolls in symmetrical balance. Later, they used motifs of sea life, including dolphins, seaweed and octopuses.

The Early Minoan Period was between 2,800 B.C. and 2,000 B.C. Their work of pottery and minor sculptures consisted of handmade clay pots with decorative geometric patterns and marble statues.

During the Middle Minoan Period, between 2,000 B.C. and approximately 1,550 B.C., Minoans built palaces for their kings and royalty, but most were destroyed during this period. With the introduction of the potter's wheel, they created delicate, thin-walled pottery often called "eggshell ware".

The Late Minoan Period, from 1,500 B.C. to 1,400 B.C., is known as the golden age of Crete. Most of the surviving Minoan work is from this time. Palaces were rebuilt with grand staircases and expansive courtyards. They even had efficient drainage systems of terra-cotta pipes. Their plastered walls were painted with frescos depicting Cretan life and nature, with bullfights, ceremonies, birds, animals, flowers and marine life.

Why the Minoan Civilization ended is still disputed. It is believed that either there was a seismic event, or the Mycenaeans took control of the peaceful island of Crete.

# Area Guide - Wood Carving

## WOOD CARVING OBJECTIVES.
Students will learn about and view Oceania wood art. Students will create, carve and paint simple geometric patterns and shapes into wood sheets. Student will depict and carve figures into wood blocks.

## SUPPLIES NEEDED.
Balsa or basswood sheets 1/4 inch or thicker, basswood carving blocks, woodcarving tools, acrylic paints, sandpaper, blank paper, drawing pencils, brushes, water, Oceania Art handout, examples of Oceania wood art (available at www.svisualart.com), movement/art worksheet, Inside Art Binder.

## MEDIA USED.
Wood
Acrylic paints

# WOOD CARVING LESSONS.

## Oceania

1. Pass out Oceania Art handout and pass out movement/art worksheet and pencils.
2. Read and discuss.
3. View examples of Oceania wood art.
4. What are some similarities in the work of the different areas? What themes do they depict?

## Carved Patterns

1. Review the characteristics of Oceania art.
   [Patterns, geometric shapes, covering the space with subdivided sections, no perspective, no modeling, the use of bright, contrasting colors.]
2. Demonstrate wood carving basics and safety.
3. Explain the project to the students. They will carve and paint, geometric patterns into the wood, subdividing sections and using other characteristics of Oceania art.
4. Pass out wood sheets, carving tools, paper and drawing pencils.
5. Students draw their ideas on paper before transferring them to the wood.
6. Students carve their wood.
7. Students paint their carvings.
8. Display and discuss student works.

## Figures in Wood

1. Demonstrate basic figure carving techniques and safety.
2. Explain the project to the students. They will carve simple figures into blocks of wood that depict dynamic poses and distorted proportions.
3. Pass out blocks of wood, paper and drawing pencils.
4. Students draw figures on paper before sculpting.
5. Students use carving tools to create their figure.
6. Display and discuss student works.

# Oceania Art

The thousands of islands between the Americas and Asia in the tropical Pacific Ocean make up what is called Oceania. Oceania art is as varied as the cultures.

POLYNESIAN

Polynesian art focused on its aristocratic society, and upholding the spiritual power [mana] of its nobility. They carved figural sculptures, very large and very small, out of stone, ivory and wood, including the enormous stone images on Easter Island. Polynesian figures were depicted in dynamic poses and were generally compact, solid and restrained.

They wore decorative bark cloth [tapa] and had a highly-developed art of tattooing. In fact, the word "tattoo" comes from Polynesia. Nobles and warriors accumulated many tattoos of geometric patterns and motifs to increase their status and their beauty.

MELANESIAN

Melanesian life was more democratic than Polynesia, and its art had many varied styles. Their art showed drama and flamboyance with intricate painting of contrasting, bright colors. People of Melanesia decorated their face and body with colorful pigments, furs, leaves, feathers and shells.

Some Melanesian artists distorted the human form using non-realistic proportions. Others painted geometric patterns that completely covered spaces. Headhunters in the area created many art forms for their rituals. A clay-like paste was applied, modeled and painted to cleaned human skulls.

AUSTRALIAN

Most of Australia's art objects were ceremonial aids. They were made to help recreate "Dream Time", their believed world creation. They used their art in reenactments of Dream Time events. They incorporated cosmic myths into songs, dances and art.

Australian art featured rhythmic repetition and fine details. They subdivided spaces and showed no perspective and no modeling. They depicted animals and humans in an x-ray-like style, showing the insides and outsides of the figure at the same time.

| PERIOD | STUDENT NAME | TOTAL POINTS | GRADE |
|---|---|---|---|
| | | | |

| LESSON POINTS | ATTENDANCE POINTS |
|---|---|
| _____ [165] | 30 - ____ = ____ <br> TOTAL MINUS DEDUCTIONS |

| LESSON | PARTICIPATION | COMPLETION | QUALITY | TOTAL POINTS |
|---|---|---|---|---|
| Geometric Human Figures | 2 4 6 8 10 | 2 4 6 8 10 | 2 4 6 8 10 | _____ |
| Animals in 3D | 2 4 6 8 10 | 2 4 6 8 10 | 2 4 6 8 10 | _____ |
| Coil Pots | 1 2 3 4 5 | 1 2 3 4 5 | 1 2 3 4 5 | _____ |
| Decorative Pots and Vases | 2 4 6 8 10 | 2 4 6 8 10 | 2 4 6 8 10 | _____ |
| Carved Patterns | 2 4 6 8 10 | 2 4 6 8 10 | 2 4 6 8 10 | _____ |
| Figures in Wood | 2 4 6 8 10 | 2 4 6 8 10 | 2 4 6 8 10 | _____ |

Participation: was the student a part of discussions, worked throughout class. Completion: student's work - did they follow directions, finish assignments. Quality: is the work carefully created, well thought-out, show self-expression.

## Attendance
Daily recording, marking late or absent and workspace/materials cleaned and stored. L=late. A=absent. ✓=clean workspace.

Legend: 8/21 | A | ✓

### ATTENDANCE DEDUCTIONS

#of Late = ____ x ____ = ____    #of Absent = ____    #of Dirty space = ____    Total = ____

### 195 TOTAL POINTS

| | |
|---|---|
| A = 195-182 | C+ = 155-151 |
| A- = 182-176 | C = 150-143 |
| | C- = 142-137 |
| B+ = 175-170 | D+ = 136-131 |
| B = 169-162 | D = 130-123 |
| B- = 161-156 | D- = 122-117 |

3D Art 1 — Grading Rubric — page 98 — VISUAL ART for the secondary grades

# 3D aRT 2: MOSaics aND eaRTH aRT

| | |
|---|---|
| Area Guide - Mosaics | page 100 |
| Mosaic Beginnings | page 100 |
| Area Guide - Earth Art | page 103 |
| Earth Art Artists | |
|    Robert Smithson | page 105 |
|    Christo | page 106 |
| Earth Art Proposal | page 107 |
| Grading Rubric | page 108 |

Area Guide - Mosaics

### INTRODUCTION.
This area covers mosaics and the Earth Art movement. Although mosaics can be considered a two-dimensional art, they do alter building interior walls, ceilings and floors. Earth Art alters sites and viewer perceptions.

### MOSAICS OBJECTIVES.
Students will learn about the beginnings of mosaics and observe ancient works. Students will create simple geometric mosaics using paper squares. Students will work together using colored pebbles and glass to compose a mosaic.

### SUPPLIES NEEDED.
Paper mosaics, black paper about 16x16 inches, glue, paper, scissors, drawing pencils, different colors of glass and pebbles, hard board panels, cement, Mosaic Art Beginnings handout, examples of mosaics (available at www.svisualart.com), movement/art worksheet (page 120), Inside Art Binder.

### MEDIA USED.
Paper mosaics
Pebble and glass mosaics

## MOSAICS LESSONS.

### The Beginnings of Mosaics

1. Pass out mosaic beginnings handout and the movement/art worksheet and pencils.
2. Read and discuss.
3. View several mosaics.
4. What are the characteristics of mosaic art from the Roman and earlier periods? Where do we see mosaics today? What themes do they show? How does the use of mosaics convey the meaning of the work?

### Geometric Mosaics

1. Review characteristics of mosaics.
2. Pass out blank paper and drawing pencils.
3. Explain the project to the students. They will create mosaics consisting of geometric shapes and patterns. They can cut squares, but only in straight lines [no curves].
4. Students draw their layout before starting with the mosaic.
5. Pass out blank black paper approximately 16x16 inches, colored paper squares and scissors.
6. Students position the squares before gluing in place.
7. Display and discuss student works.

### Class Mosaic

This lesson used colored pebbles and glass to create a large mosaic. With the cement and the size of the mosaic, it can become heavy very quickly. Be sure to use panels to reduce the weight and size. Mosaics need to be flat to work on and dry as well.

1. Decide on an image [landscape or still life] that the class will use as a reference to create a mosaic. This can be a photograph showing a local scene or an image off the internet.
2. Using hardboard, create several panels. Use a size appropriate for your classroom, but try for at least three feet tall by 5 feet wide.
3. Draw outlines of colored areas onto the board.
4. Students decide on colors to use in each area and start applying pebbles and glass to the hardboard. [Glue or cement can be used.]
5. Allow mosaic to dry and cement to set. Grout around the tiles and seal.
6. Display mosaic and discuss the process.

# Mosaic Art Beginnings

During the eighth century B.C., floor mosaics began appearing in the Mediterranean region. Mosaics were a durable and inexpensive floor covering that could be used in place of carpet. They were geometric patterns of small collected pebbles set in thick cement. In the fourth century B.C., more complex pictorial designs made of rich colors were replacing the patterns.

The use of pebbles to create mosaics was popular through the Roman times. By the second century B.C., they started using blue, red and green colored glass as well.

Mosaics began being applied to Roman walls around the first century A.D. These mosaics showed great detail through minute workmanship and their goal was to copy painting techniques of the time. They depicted a range of themes including classical mythology, historical subjects, rural themes, chariot races, the theater, gladiatorial battles and hunting. Many themes were taken from the works of the Greeks.

During the second and third centuries A.D., strong color effects could be achieved on the wall mosaics. They used glass paste and enamel since they didn't need the durability required for floor mosaics. Many Roman mosaics used striking reds and blacks, delicate greens and tans, blue accents and creamy whites.

Under Constantine, during the early Christian period, mosaics were placed high on church walls and apse vaults. Meant to be seen from a distance, they didn't need the minute detail of earlier Roman works. The mosaics were in brilliant color, as the use of reflective glass became standard. Often, mosaics would cover the entire interior walls of the buildings.

## EARTH ART OBJECTIVES.
Students will explore and discuss the Earth Art movement. Students will learn about Christo and Robert Smithson, including their lives and their art. Students will work together to create their own Earth Art, complete with sketches and plans.

## EARTH ART OVERVIEW.
Started in the late 1960s, the Earth Art movement has also been called Site Art and Land Art. Artists worked to reawaken sensory perceptions of viewers to their natural and urban environments. Their art would be sometimes produced in remote areas that could be viewed only by photographs. Other art modified urban areas and lasted for short periods of time. Earth Art started in America, but has progressed throughout the world, and many installations can still be seen and are still being created.

## SUPPLIES NEEDED.
Sites around campus, natural and modern materials, Christo and Robert Smithson handouts, examples of their work (available at www.svisualart.com), Earth Art proposal worksheet, permission to install art around the school, movement/art worksheet (page 120), Inside Art Binder.

## MEDIA USED.
Earth, natural and modern materials

# Area Guide - Earth Art

## EARTH ART LESSONS.

### About the Artists - Christo and Smithson

1. Introduce and discuss the Earth Art movement and pass out movement/art worksheet and pencils.
2. Pass out Christo handout, read and discuss.
3. View and discuss Christo's art.
4. Pass out Robert Smithson handout, read and discuss.
5. View and discuss Smithosn's art.
6. Compare the works of Christo and Smithson. What elements and principles of art did they use? Should their works be considered art? Why?

### Altering the Landscape

1. Assemble the students into groups of four or five.
2. Explain the project to the students. They will create an Earth Art work using natural materials to form sculpture or alter the natural landscape with modern found materials. Their art needs to be non-toxic and non-permanent to the environment.
3. Pass out the Earth Art proposal worksheet and discuss requirements and steps.
4. Tour the exterior and interior sites available for the students to place their art.
5. Students plan and sketch their ideas, choosing one idea to prepare and present to the teacher for approval.
6. Upon approval, students gather materials and assemble their work.
7. Tour sites with students presenting their work and describing the process they used. Take photographs of all work.
8. Students dismantle art and return sites to their original look.
9. Discuss the creation and viewer reactions to the students' Earth Art.

# ROBERT SMITHSON
[1938-1973] America

Robert Smithson was born in New Jersey and studied for two years at the Art Students League in New York, starting in 1953. He also studied briefly in 1956 at the Brooklyn Museum School. In 1959, Smithson taught art and had his first one man show of his paintings in New York.

He worked mainly as a painter until 1964, when he started writing and sculpting. In 1966, Smithson began working with outside materials, creating what he called "non-sites". He would create a scene in an outdoor place, take aerial photographs and then display those photographs. He also would move outdoor materials to museums, displaying them in metal tins and with topographical maps and photographs.

Smithson soon moved to large-scale outdoor projects, and did a series of modifying existing landscapes. In 1970, he tried to unify art and nature by creating a vast coil of earth and stone out into the Great Salt Lake in Utah. It is called the "Spiral Jetty" and the coil is 1,500 feet long and 15 feet wide. He recorded its construction in film and photographs, and most viewers have only seen the Jetty through photographs. It is still there, but difficult to get to, and is not always visible due to seasonal shifts in the water level of the lake.

In addition to recording his projects in film and photography, Smithson wrote many articles and essays on his art. While studying the site for his "Amarillo Ramp" in Texas, he died in a plane crash at the age of 35. His widow completed the ramp with his notes and drawings. Some of his outdoor projects still exist and are available to visit.

# CHRISTO [KREE-stoh]
## [1935- ] Bulgaria

Christo studied at the Fine Arts Academy in Sofia from 1953 through 1956. He then spent six months in Prague, but escaped from the Russian Communism there. He went to Vienna, and then to Paris in 1958.

He began encasing objects like tin cans, bottles, stacks of magazines, furniture and cars in clumsy wrappings. Christo wanted to make them look like unopened packages.

Starting in 1961, Christo began collaborating with his wife, Jeanne-Claude. They moved to New York in 1964, where they wrapped sections of buildings and storefronts, and eventually entire buildings. Together, they work to modify urban sites with cloth.

Christo soon switched to modifying natural sites. He created a hanging curtain of orange nylon, 417 meters wide, across a canyon, and wrapped one million square feet of Australian coast. In 1983, he surrounded eleven small man-made islands with pink polypropylene fabric for just two weeks. It took two years of preparation, $3.2 million, and 600,000 square meters of fabric. Crowds gathered and watched Christo and his crew first surround the islands and then unfold the large cloth.

Each project requires years of preparation, research and meetings with local authorities and community members. Christo raises money for his creations through the sale of drawings and collages made to visualize parts of the projects. He usually documents the process as well. Christo and his wife continue to collaborate and live in New York.

# GROUP PROPOSAL

Name _____

Group Members: _____

Our top 3 Earth Art ideas:

1. _____

2. _____

3. _____

Preferred site:

1. _____  2. _____  3. _____

Approved Site:
_____

Approved Idea:
_____

Date: _____ Teacher Signature: _____

Materials Needed:
_____
_____
_____

Description of Site and Art:
_____
_____
_____
_____
_____
_____
_____
_____
_____

| PERIOD | STUDENT NAME | | TOTAL POINTS | GRADE |
|---|---|---|---|---|

**LESSON POINTS** _____ [105]

**ATTENDANCE POINTS** 30 - ____ = ____
TOTAL MINUS DEDUCTIONS

| LESSON | PARTICIPATION | COMPLETION | QUALITY | TOTAL POINTS |
|---|---|---|---|---|
| Geometric Mosaics | 2 4 6 8 10 | 2 4 6 8 10 | 2 4 6 8 10 | _____ |
| Class Mosaic | 2 4 6 8 10 | 2 4 6 8 10 | 2 4 6 8 10 | _____ |
| Altering the Landscape — Earth Art Proposal | 1 2 3 4 5 | 1 2 3 4 5 | 1 2 3 4 5 | _____ |
| Installation and Presentation | 2 4 6 8 10 | 2 4 6 8 10 | 2 4 6 8 10 | _____ |

Participation: was the student a part of discussions, worked throughout class. Completion: student's work - did they follow directions, finish assignments. Quality: is the work carefully created, well thought-out, show self-expression.

## Attendance
Daily recording, marking late or absent and workspace/materials cleaned and stored. L=late. A=absent. ✓=clean workspace.

8/21
A
✓

**ATTENDANCE DEDUCTIONS**

#of Late = ____ x ____ = ____  #of Absent = ____  #of Dirty space = ____  Total = ____

**135 TOTAL POINTS**

| | |
|---|---|
| A = 135-126 | C+ = 107-104 |
| A- = 125-122 | C = 103-99 |
| | C- = 98-95 |
| B+ = 121-118 | D+ = 94-91 |
| B = 117-112 | D = 90-85 |
| B- = 111-108 | D- = 84-81 |

3D Art 2 — Grading Rubric — VISUAL ART for the secondary grades

# analysis & portfolio

| | |
|---|---|
| Area Guide | page 110 |
| Area Worksheets | |
|    Discussing Art | page 113 |
|    About My Art | page 114 |
|    My Style | page 115 |
| Grading Rubric | page 116 |

# Area Guide - Analysis and Portfolio

## AREA OBJECTIVES.
Students will collect and keep their works throughout the year. Students will analyze the work of well-known artists and their own works regarding aesthetic values and the elements and principles of art. Students will describe their own style and what media they prefer to work with. Students will choose one of their previous works to refine and rework. Students will prepare a final portfolio of their work that demonstrates their style, skills and a variety of media.

## AREA OVERVIEW.
It is important for students to be able to discuss art using the language of the visual arts. They will use their Inside Art Binders to help them describe art by well-known artists as well as their own work, critiquing, writing and presenting their findings and conclusions. A portfolio of their work should be kept throughout the year, and can be used to help students get into art programs or work in the arts.

## SUPPLIES NEEDED.
Large folder for containing art, lined and blank paper, drawing pencils, canvas or other surface material, various media [student choice], brushes, student's work, discussing art, about my art and my style worksheets, Inside Art Binder, examples of well-known artists' work.

## ANALYSIS LESSONS.

### Discussing Art
1. Students choose one artist and their work that was covered throughout the year.
2. Pass out "Discussing Art" worksheet and discuss the assignment. They should use their Inside Art Binder to help fillout the worksheet.
3. Students complete the worksheet and use it to write an essay about their artist's works of art.
4. Students present their findings and conclusions.

### About My Art
1. Students retreive their portfolios and select three works that represent their best work.
2. Pass out three copies of "About My Art" worksheet to each student and discuss the assignment. They should use their Inside Art Binder to help them.
3. Students complete the worksheet and use it to write an essay about their works.

### Finding My Style
1. Students retreive their portfolios.
2. Pass out "My Style" worksheet and discuss.
3. Students analyze their works, determining what elements and principles of art are most dominant to their works. What they believe is their personal style, and what media they prefer to use.
4. Students complete the worksheet and write an essay.

### Refining One Work
1. Students retreive their portfolios.
2. They choose one piece that they want to rework and improve, in their own style, or using different media.
3. Students use their choice of media and sketch their work before painting.
4. Display original and new student works.
5. Students present their work and describe why they chose that piece and how they refined it.

Area Guide - Analysis and Portfolio

# PORTFOLIO LESSONS.

## Saving Works

1. After completing art creation lessons, including displaying of works, students save work to a portfolio. A large folder should be used.
2. Students continue to put works into their portfolios throughout the year.

## Final Portfolios

1. Students retreive their portfolios.
2. They select 10-15 of their best pieces, works that show their style and skills.
3. Other works can be taken home or given away.
4. Students display their choosen works and present them to the class.
5. Students keep their portfolios for future use. [i.e. - another art class, postsecondary education, job application, etc.]

# Discussing Art

Name _____

Artist: _____

Elements of Art used and how they are used:

_____
_____
_____
_____
_____
_____
_____
_____

Principles of Art used and how they are used:

_____
_____
_____
_____
_____
_____
_____
_____

Are this artist's works aesthetically pleasing? Why or why not?

_____
_____
_____
_____
_____
_____
_____
_____

| Visual Art for the secondary grades | page 113 | Analysis & Portfolio | Discussing Art |

# ABOUT MY ART

Name _____

Title of work: _____

Media used: _____

What is the intent of the work? Why did you create it and how?
_____
_____
_____
_____
_____
_____
_____

Elements of Art used and how they are used:
_____
_____
_____
_____
_____
_____
_____
_____

Principles of Art used and how they are used:
_____
_____
_____
_____
_____
_____
_____
_____

# MY STYLE

Name _____

**What elements did you use and how?**

_____
_____
_____
_____
_____
_____
_____

**What principles did you use and how?**

_____
_____
_____
_____
_____
_____
_____

**Media you prefer to use and why:**

_____
_____
_____
_____
_____
_____

**What is you style?**

_____
_____
_____
_____
_____
_____

| VISUAL ART for the secondary grades | page 115 | Analysis & Portfolio | Finding My Style |

| PERIOD | STUDENT NAME | TOTAL POINTS | GRADE |
|---|---|---|---|
| | | | |

| LESSON POINTS | ATTENDANCE POINTS |
|---|---|
| _____ [120] | 30 - ____ = _____ TOTAL MINUS DEDUCTIONS |

| LESSON | PARTICIPATION | COMPLETION | QUALITY | TOTAL POINTS |
|---|---|---|---|---|
| Discussing Art | 1 2 3 4 5 | 1 2 3 4 5 | 1 2 3 4 5 | _____ |
| About My Art | 2 4 6 8 10 | 2 4 6 8 10 | 2 4 6 8 10 | _____ |
| Finding My Style | 1 2 3 4 5 | 1 2 3 4 5 | 1 2 3 4 5 | _____ |
| Refining One Work | 2 4 6 8 10 | 2 4 6 8 10 | 2 4 6 8 10 | _____ |
| Final Portfolios | 2 4 6 8 10 | 2 4 6 8 10 | 2 4 6 8 10 | _____ |

Participation: was the student a part of discussions, worked throughout class. Completion: student's work - did they follow directions, finish assignments. Quality: is the work carefully created, well thought-out, show self-expression.

## Attendance
Daily recording marking late or absent and workspace/materials cleaned and stored. L=late. A=absent. ✓=clean workspace.

8/21
A
✓

### ATTENDANCE DEDUCTIONS
#of Late = ____ x ____ = ____    #of Absent = ____    #of Dirty space = ____    Total = ____

### 150 TOTAL POINTS
| | |
|---|---|
| A = 150-140 | C+ = 119-116 |
| A- = 139-135 | C = 115-110 |
| | C- = 109-105 |
| B+ = 134-131 | D+ = 104-101 |
| B = 130-125 | D = 100-95 |
| B- = 124-120 | D- = 94-90 |

Analysis & Portfolio    Grading Rubric    VISUAL ART for the secondary grades

# appendix

Timeline of Artists . . . . . . . . . . . . . . . . . . . . . . . . . . . . . . . . . . . . . . . . . page 118

Index of Artists . . . . . . . . . . . . . . . . . . . . . . . . . . . . . . . . . . . . . . . . . . page 119

Movement/Art Worksheet . . . . . . . . . . . . . . . . . . . . . . . . . . . . . . . . . . page 120

References . . . . . . . . . . . . . . . . . . . . . . . . . . . . . . . . . . . . . . . . . . . . page 121

State Standards Addressed . . . . . . . . . . . . . . . . . . . . . . . . . . . . . . . . . page 122

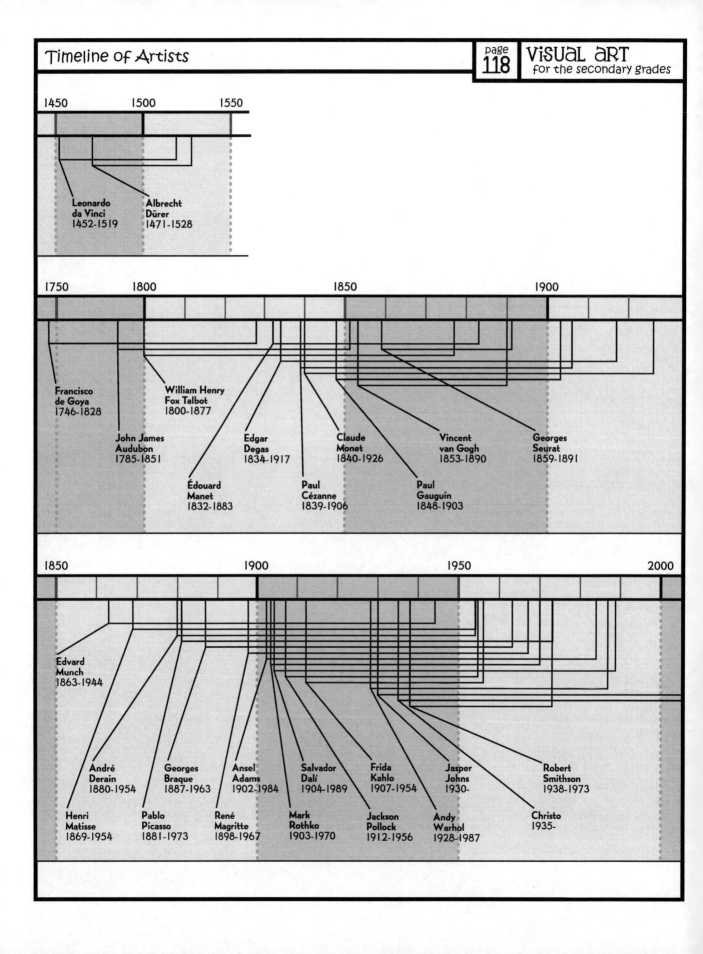

# Index of Artists

|  | LESSON, HANDOUT |
|---|---|
| Adams, Ansel | 86, 89 |
| Audubon, John James | 39, 41 |
| Braque, Georges | 61, 63 |
| Cézanne, Paul | 48, 51 |
| Christo | 104, 106 |
| Dalí, Salvador | 65, 67 |
| Degas, Edgar | 43, 47 |
| Derain, André | 57, 58 |
| Dürer, Albrecht | 29, 35 |
| Gauguin, Paul | 48, 53 |
| Gogh, Vincent van | 48, 52 |
| Goya, Francisco de | 39, 40 |
| Johns, Jasper | 76, 79 |
| Kahlo, Frida | 65, 68 |
| Leonardo da Vinci | 29, 34 |
| Magritte, René | 65, 69 |
| Manet, Édouard | 43, 45 |
| Matisse, Henri | 57, 59 |
| Monet, Claude | 43, 46 |
| Munch, Edvard | 82, 84 |
| Picasso, Pablo | 61, 62 |
| Pollock, Jackson | 73, 74 |
| Rothko, Mark | 73, 74 |
| Seurat, Georges | 48, 50 |
| Smithson, Robert | 104, 105 |
| Talbot, William Henry Fox | 86, 88 |
| Warhol, Andy | 76, 78 |

# MOVEMENT/ART

Name _____

Movement/Type of Art: _____

Description:
_____
_____
_____
_____
_____
_____

Artists:
_____
_____
_____
_____

Important Works:
_____
_____
_____
_____

Characteristics, Themes, Techniques of the Movement/Type of Art:
_____
_____
_____
_____
_____
_____

Appendix | Movement/Artist | VISUAL ART for the secondary grades

## Articles

Amory, Dita. *Georges Seurat [1859-1891] and Neo-Impressionism.* In Heilbrunn Timeline of Art History. [October 2004]. New York: The Metropolitan Museum of Art, 2000-.

Auricchio, Laura. *Claude Monet [1840-1926].* In Heilbrunn Timeline of Art History. [October 2004]. New York: The Metropolitan Museum of Art, 2000-.

Bambach, Carmen. *Leonardo da Vinci [1452-1519].* In Heilbrunn Timeline of Art History. [October 2002]. New York: The Metropolitan Museum of Art, 2000-.

Dabrowski, Magdalena. *Henri Matisse [1869-1954].* In Heilbrunn Timeline of Art History. [October 2004]. New York: The Metropolitan Museum of Art, 2000-.

Daniel, Malcolm. *William Henry Fox Talbot [1800-1877] and the Invention of Photography.* In Heilbrunn Timeline of Art History. [October 2004]. New York: The Metropolitan Museum of Art, 2000-.

Department of Nineteenth-Century, Modern, and Contemporary Art. *Vincent van Gogh [1853-1890].* In Heilbrunn Timeline of Art History. [October 2004, revised March 2010]. New York: The Metropolitan Museum of Art, 2000-.

Rabinow, Rebecca. *Edouard Manet [1832-1883].* In Heilbrunn Timeline of Art History. [October 2004]. New York: The Metropolitan Museum of Art, 2000-.

Rosenthal, Nan. *Jasper Johns [born 1930].* In Heilbrunn Timeline of Art History. [October 2004]. New York: The Metropolitan Museum of Art, 2000-.

Schenkel, Ruth. *Edgar Degas [1834-1917]: Painting and Drawing.* In Heilbrunn Timeline of Art History. [October 2004]. New York: The Metropolitan Museum of Art, 2000-.

Voorhies, James. *Francisco de Goya {1746-1828] and the Spanish Enlightenment.* In Heilbrunn Timeline of Art History. [October 2003]. New York: The Metropolitan Museum of Art, 2000-.

Voorhies, James. *Pablo Picasso [1881-1973].* In Heilbrunn Timeline of Art History. [October 2004]. New York: The Metropolitan Museum of Art, 2000-.

Voorhies, James. *Paul Cézanne [1839-1906].* In Heilbrunn Timeline of Art History. [October 2004]. New York: The Metropolitan Museum of Art, 2000-.

## Books

Belvin, Marjorie Elliott. *Design Through Discovery,* fourth edition. [1985]. New York: Holt Rinehart Winston, Inc.

Canaday, John. *Mainstreams in Modern Art,* second edition. [1981]. Fort Worth, Texas: Harcourt Brace Jovanovich College Publishers.

*Color Harmony Workbook.* [1994]. Gloucester, Massachusetts: Rockport Publishers, Inc.

De la Croix, Hurst., Richard G. Tansey and Diane Kirkpatrick. *Gardner's Art Through the Ages,* nineth edition. [1991]. Fort Worth, Texas: Harcourt Brace Jovanovich College Publishers.

Honnef, Klaus. *Andy Warhol.* [1990]. West Germany. Benedikt Taschen Verlag GmbH and Co, KG.

*Jasper Johns.* [1997]. Italy: Universe Publishing.

*Matisse - 50 Years of His Graphic Art.* [1956]. New York: George Braziller, Inc.

Meuris, Jacques. *Magritte.* [1988]. New York: Artabras Publishers.

Myers, Bernard S. and Trewin Copperston. *The History of Art.* [1990]. Yugoslavia: Dorset Press.

## Websites

www.anseladams.com

www.artlex.com

www.audubon.com

www.barewalls.com

www.dickblick.com

www.dictionary.com

www.freestylephoto.biz

www.fridakahlo.com

www.jacksonpollock.com

www.metmuseum.org

www.moma.org

cde.ca.gov

munch.museum.no

# California Standards

## Visual Art for the secondary grades

### Color Theory

A 1.1 Analyze and discuss complex ideas, such as distortion, color theory, arbitrary color, scale, expressive content, and real versus virtual in works of art.

### Elements and Principles of Art

P 1.1 Identify and use the principles of design to discuss, analyze, and write about visual aspects in the environment and in works of art, including their own.

P 2.1 Solve a visual arts problem that involves the effective use of the elements of art and the principles of design.

### Drawing

P 2.4 Review and refine observational drawing skills.

A 1.1 Analyze and discuss complex ideas, such as distortion, color theory, arbitrary color, scale, expressive content, and real versus virtual in works of art.

### Realism

P 1.3 Research and analyze the work of an artist and write about the artist's distinctive style and its contribution to the meaning of the work.

P 4.1 Articulate how personal beliefs, cultural traditions, and current social, economic, and political contexts influence the interpretation of the meaning or message in a work of art.

P 4.2 Compare the ways in which meaning of a specific work of art has been affected over time because of changes in interpretation and context.

A 1.1 Analyze and discuss complex ideas, such as distortion, color theory, arbitrary color, scale, expressive content, and real versus virtual in works of art.

A 2.3 Assemble and display objects of works of art as a part of a public exhibition.

A 4.1 Describe the relationship involving the art maker [artist], the making [process], the artwork [products], and the viewer.

A 4.3 Analyze and articulate how society influences the interpretation and message of a work of art.

### Impressionism

P 2.1 Solve a visual arts problem that involves the effective use of the elements of art and the principles of design.

A 1.4 Research two periods of painting, sculpture, film, or other media and discuss their similarities and differences, using the language of the visual arts.

A 2.2 Plan and create works of art that reflect complex ideas, such as distortion, color theory, arbitrary color, scale, expressive content, and real versus virtual.

A 2.3 Assemble and display objects of works of art as a part of a public exhibition.

A 2.5 Use innovative visual metaphors in creating works of art.

A 4.1 Describe the relationship involving the art maker [artist], the making [process], the artwork [products], and the viewer.

### Post Impressionism

P 1.3 Research and analyze the work of an artist and write about the artist's distinctive style and its contribution to the meaning of the work.

P 1.4 Analyze and describe how the composition of a work of art is affected by the use of a particular principle of design.

P 2.1 Solve a visual arts problem that involves the effective use of the elements of art and the principles of design.

P 2.5 Create an expressive composition, focusing on dominance and subordination.

A 1.1 Analyze and discuss complex ideas, such as distortion, color theory, arbitrary color, scale, expressive content, and real versus virtual in works of art.

A 1.4 Research two periods of painting, sculpture, film, or other media and discuss their similarities and differences, using the language of the visual arts.

A 1.6 Describe the use of the elements of art to express mood in one or more of their works of art.

A 2.2 Plan and create works of art that reflect complex ideas, such as distortion, color theory, arbitrary color, scale, expressive content, and real versus virtual.

A 2.3 Assemble and display objects of works of art as a part of a public exhibition.

### Fauvism

P 2.4 Review and refine observational drawing skills.

A 1.1 Analyze and discuss complex ideas, such as distortion, color theory, arbitrary color, scale, expressive content, and real versus virtual in works of art.

A 1.4 Research two periods of painting, sculpture, film, or other media and discuss their similarities and differences, using the language of the visual arts.

A 1.6 Describe the use of the elements of art to express mood in one or more of their works of art.

A 2.3 Assemble and display objects of works of art as a part of a public exhibition.

### Cubism

P 2.1 Solve a visual arts problem that involves the effective use of the elements of art and the principles of design.

A 1.8 Analyze the works of a well-known artist as to the art media selected and the effect of that selection on the artist's style.

A 2.2 Plan and create works of art that reflect complex ideas, such as distortion, color theory, arbitrary color, scale, expressive content, and real versus virtual.

A 2.3 Assemble and display objects of works of art as a part of a public exhibition.

### Surrealism

P 1.5 Analyze the material used by a given artist and describe how its use influences the meaning of the work.

P 2.1 Solve a visual arts problem that involves the effective use of the elements of art and the principles of design.

A 1.1 Analyze and discuss complex ideas, such as distortion, color theory, arbitrary color, scale, expressive content, and real versus virtual in works of art.

A 2.1 Create original works of art of increasing complexity and skill in a variety of media that reflect their feelings and points of view.

A 2.2 Plan and create works of art that reflect complex ideas, such as distortion, color theory, arbitrary color, scale, expressive content, and real versus virtual.

A 2.3 Assemble and display objects of works of art as a part of a public exhibition.

A 2.4 Demonstrate in their own works of art a personal style and advanced proficiency in communicating an idea, theme or emotion.

A 2.5 Use innovative visual metaphors in creating works of art.

### Contemporary Art

P 3.2 Identify and describe the role and influence of new technologies on contemporary works of art.

P 3.3 Identify and describe trends in the visual arts and discuss how the issues of time, place, and cultural influence are reflected in selected works of art.

P 3.4 Discuss the purposes of art in selected contemporary cultures.

A 2.1 Create original works of art of increasing complexity and skill in a variety of media that reflect their feelings and points of view.

A 2.2 Plan and create works of art that reflect complex ideas, such as distortion, color theory, arbitrary color, scale, expressive content, and real versus virtual.

A 2.3 Assemble and display objects of works of art as a part of a public exhibition.

A 2.4 Demonstrate in their own works of art a personal style and advanced proficiency in communicating an idea, theme or emotion.

A 3.1 Identify contemporary styles and discuss the diverse social, economic, and political developments reflected in the works of art examined.

# Visual Art for the secondary grades — page 123 — California Standards

A 3.2 Identify contemporary artists world-wide who have achieved regional, national, or international recognition and discuss ways in which their work reflects, plays a role in, and influences present-day culture.

A 4.2 Identify the intentions of artists creating contemporary works of art and explore the implications of those intentions.

## Pop Art

P 1.5 Analyze the material used by a given artist and describe how its use influences the meaning of the work.

P 3.2 Identify and describe the role and influence of new technologies on contemporary works of art.

A 1.1 Analyze and discuss complex ideas, such as distortion, color theory, arbitrary color, scale, expressive content, and real versus virtual in works of art.

A 1.8 Analyze the works of a well-known artist as to the art media selected and the effect of that selection on the artist's style.

A 2.2 Plan and create works of art that reflect complex ideas, such as distortion, color theory, arbitrary color, scale, expressive content, and real versus virtual.

A 2.3 Assemble and display objects of works of art as a part of a public exhibition.

A 2.4 Demonstrate in their own works of art a personal style and advanced proficiency in communicating an idea, theme or emotion.

A 3.1 Identify contemporary styles and discuss the diverse social, economic, and political developments reflected in the works of art examined.

A 3.2 Identify contemporary artists world-wide who have achieved regional, national, or international recognition and discuss ways in which their work reflects, plays a role in, and influences present-day culture.

A 5.1 Speculate on how advances in technology might change the definition and function of the visual arts.

A 5.2 Compare and contrast works of art, probing beyond the obvious and identifying psychological content found in the symbols and images.

## Printmaking

P 2.4 Review and refine observational drawing skills.

A 2.1 Create original works of art of increasing complexity and skill in a variety of media that reflect their feelings and points of view.

A 2.3 Assemble and display objects of works of art as a part of a public exhibition.

A 2.6 Present a universal concept in a multimedia work of art that demonstrates knowledge of technology skills.

## Photography

P 1.5 Analyze the material used by a given artist and describe how its use influences the meaning of the work.

P 2.1 Solve a visual arts problem that involves the effective use of the elements of art and the principles of design.

A 1.6 Describe the use of the elements of art to express mood in one or more of their works of art.

A 1.8 Analyze the works of a well-known artist as to the art media selected and the effect of that selection on the artist's style.

A 2.2 Plan and create works of art that reflect complex ideas, such as distortion, color theory, arbitrary color, scale, expressive content, and real versus virtual.

A 2.3 Assemble and display objects of works of art as a part of a public exhibition.

## Pottery

A 2.2 Plan and create works of art that reflect complex ideas, such as distortion, color theory, arbitrary color, scale, expressive content, and real versus virtual.

A 2.3 Assemble and display objects of works of art as a part of a public exhibition.

A 3.3 Investigate and discuss universal concepts expressed in works of art from diverse cultures.

## Wood Carving

A 2.2 Plan and create works of art that reflect complex ideas, such as distortion, color theory, arbitrary color, scale, expressive content, and real versus virtual.

A 2.3 Assemble and display objects of works of art as a part of a public exhibition.

A 3.2 Identify contemporary artists world-wide who have achieved regional, national, or international recognition and discuss ways in which their work reflects, plays a role in, and influences present-day culture.

## Mosaics

P 1.5 Analyze the material used by a given artist and describe how its use influences the meaning of the work.

P 2.1 Solve a visual arts problem that involves the effective use of the elements of art and the principles of design.

A 1.8 Analyze the works of a well-known artist as to the art media selected and the effect of that selection on the artist's style.

## Earth Art

P 1.1 Identify and use the principles of design to discuss, analyze, and write about visual aspects in the environment and in works of art, including their own.

P 2.1 Solve a visual arts problem that involves the effective use of the elements of art and the principles of design.

A 2.2 Plan and create works of art that reflect complex ideas, such as distortion, color theory, arbitrary color, scale, expressive content, and real versus virtual.

A 2.3 Assemble and display objects of works of art as a part of a public exhibition.

A 4.1 Describe the relationship involving the art maker [artist], the making [process], the artwork [products], and the viewer.

A 4.5 Construct a rationale for the validity of a specific work of art - artwork that falls outside their own conceptions of art.

## Analysis and Portfolio Development

P 2.2 Prepare a portfolio of original two- and three-dimensional works of art that reflects refined craftsmanship and technical skills.

P 4.3 Formulate and support a position regarding the aesthetic value of a specific work of art and change or defend that position after considering the views of others.

P 4.4 Articulate the process and rationale for refining and reworking one of their own works of art.

P 4.5 Employ the conventions of art criticism in writing and speaking about works of art.

A 1.2 Discuss a series of their original works of art, using the appropriate vocabulary of art.

A 1.3 Analyze their works of art as to personal direction and style.

A 1.7 Select three works of art from their art portfolio and discuss the intent of the work and the use of the media.

A 4.4 Apply various art-related theoretical perspectives to their own works of art and the work of others in classroom critiques.

A 4.6 Develop written criteria for the selection of a body of work from their portfolios that represents significant achievements.

A 5.3 Prepare portfolios of their original works of art for a variety of purposes [e.g., review for postsecondary application, exhibition, job application, and personal collection].

---

P = Proficient level that can be achieved at the end of the first year of visual art education in grades nine through twelve.

A = Advanced level that can be achieved at the end of the second year of visual art education in grades nine through twelve.

Visit www.tahoekerri.com to learn about other books by Kerrian Neu, and to purchase books and other materials.

Made in the USA
Middletown, DE
31 May 2025